T0099901

Martha Washington's Quilt

A Quilted Story

Jean Crawford

WestBow
PRESS
A DIVISION OF THOMAS NELSON

ISBN: 978-1-4497-5459-4 (sc)
ISBN: 978-1-4497-5460-0 (e)

Library of Congress Control Number: 2012909670

WestBow Press books may be ordered through booksellers or by contacting:

WestBow Press
A Division of Thomas Nelson
1663 Liberty Drive
Bloomington, IN 47403
www.westbowpress.com
1-(866) 928-1240

Because of the dynamic nature of the Internet, any web addresses or links contained in this book may have changed since publication and may no longer be valid. The views expressed in this work are solely those of the author and do not necessarily reflect the views of the publisher, and the publisher hereby disclaims any responsibility for them. Any people depicted in stock imagery provided by Thinkstock are models, and such images are being used for illustrative purposes only.

Certain stock imagery © Thinkstock.

Printed in the United States of America

WestBow Press rev. date: 06/18/12

Martha Washington's Quilt is dedicated to Eleanor Peck with a heart-felt THANK-YOU.

I came to know Eleanor while living in Deltona, Florida. She and her husband previously served in the Missionary Home Station of Brazil to maintain a "home away from home" for the Missionaries serving in the jungle areas. Eleanor was kind enough to share a copy of her family's genealogy with me.

This book is based on her family's genealogy.

TABLE OF CONTENTS

ACKNOWLEDGEMENTS

THIS PAST YEAR AND the completion of my latest book, Martha Washington's Quilt, has been a journey and accomplishment I could not have completed on my own. Today and always I must first acknowledge and thank the Lord for being with me every step of the way.

"The Lord is my rock, my fortress and my deliverer; my God is my rock in whom I take my refuge. He is my shield and the horn of my salvation, my stronghold." (Psalm 18:2)

My husband of 62 years, Jim, passed away on May 6, 2011. How I miss him - the conversations we had as well as his encouragement, interest, and his love of my writing and all my ongoing projects.

My family encouraged me as I continued with this project of writing about our Colonies and their construction during the time period of the Revolutionary War.

My daughter, Nanci Crawford, proofread the manuscript and gave me many helpful ideas.

My sister, Louise Kraft, wrote the beautiful poem that concludes this book.

Thank you to all my readers for their encouraging letters and comments about the previous books I have written.

Your words mean so much.

- Jean Crawford

INTRODUCTION

NOVA SCOTIA AND CONNECTICUT have a mutual interest in the Colony's freedom even to the point of Nova Scotia considering joining as the fourteenth colony. The Quilted Story, Martha Washington's Quilt, will bring attention to little known pieces of history through the life of the Starr family and their family member, Samuel Huntington who signed the Declaration of Independence, putting his life on the line as well as the other signers, when they revolted against Great Britain and King George.

More important to the story you are about to read is this: the first shots of the American Revolutionary War rang out on April 19, 1775 at what is known as the Battle of Lexington and Concord. These battles were the official beginning of the armed conflict between the Kingdom of Great Britain and its 13 colonies in what was then the mainland of British North America. And when those shots rang out, many people and the lives of many families were forever changed. Martha Washington's Quilt is the story of one Connecticut family with ties to their Nova Scotia family who lived through one of our nation's most trying times. As you turn the pages of the story and come to know the Starr family, I hope you will feel their pain, their joy, their challenges, their triumphs, and mostly their love for each other. Because given a different time and circumstance, their story could be yours.

Chapter i

Pirate Danger at Sea

It would soon be time to harvest the apples this September of 1775. The smell of apples permeated the air and the sound of the apples picked abounded through the orchard with the sweet voices of the children as they gathered them along with their parents. The bells ringing provided the background for the apple production. You could hear the bells stop ringing when the children stopped picking while they played tag among the trees only to be reprimanded by their parents to start picking again. It was a project for the mothers to make the baskets during the winter. They put the false bottoms in which hid the bell in the bottom of the basket. Joseph loved this time of year. As he sat on the veranda of his home in Nova Scotia he wondered how he could stand to leave.

How could he leave all this just to further his education? He could see parts of the orchards in the distance. He always enjoyed the harvest. How he loved to taste the cider. The whole family joined to make the delicious drink. He supposed his Papa would be out from the orchard to talk to him again. He knew there was no use fighting it. He certainly didn't want to be disrespectful to his father but he didn't want to go to college. He just wanted to be a farmer and follow in his father's footsteps. He loved to be outdoors and the only other interest he had was to join his friends in the Sons of Liberty. They were still trying to get George Washington to help them organize a group to help in this rumored war.

The sun was going down and David Starr was coming up the walk. He had worked in the orchards all day. He noticed Joseph on the veranda. "I could have used your help today, son," he said. He knew Joseph wanted to spend his life working on the farm and in the orchards. His dream for his son was to study at the university and become a lawyer. His nephew, Samuel had studied on his own, borrowed books and helped his father farm the land while he studied any moment he could find. He became a lawyer, a Judge and at the present time was a delegate from Connecticut to the General Congress.

"I would have been happy to help out in the orchard, Papa. I knew I would be leaving tonight to board the sloop to go to Connecticut. I wanted to have everything packed up ready to go. Mother helped me and I helped her start the supper. Papa, I would be so happy if you would change your mind and let me stay home. I love to work in the orchards."

David climbed the steps to the veranda where his son and daughter were visiting. Joseph favored David's side of the family. His black hair and height of six feet told everyone that they were father and son. They had always worked well together and David knew he would certainly miss his son. He was so proud of him but he knew he was capable of doing more than working on their land. He could be a lawyer and even work in the government if he had the right education. He knew Joseph would be safe with his relatives in Connecticut. The Starrs even had children about the same age as Joseph. He knew Joanna was only a couple years younger. If they only could get him on that sloop safely tonight. You never knew where the pirates were hanging out. Then there was always trouble between tradesmen of the colonies and England.

"Let's not talk about that right now, Joseph. Let's just enjoy our supper tonight. It certainly smells good. I suppose we are having your favorite foods to eat for this meal." David shook some of the dirt off his shoes and brushed off his knickers before entering the house. His sweet wife, Susannah was finishing setting the table. "I guess you were busy all day with this meal, sweetheart," he said as he walked over to the table to give her a hug.

"To tell the truth, David, I feel more like mourning than celebrating today. I will miss him so much. It seems like our children have just grown up too fast. I was thinking all day of all the things that have happened since he was born. I wish he could stay and help in the orchards and the fields as he wishes. I understand that he needs to grow up and be independent from us but it grieves me that he is leaving and it is so dangerous, honey….so dangerous…. having to leave at night and all those pirate ships that they could encounter. I certainly will not sleep one wink tonight," she said as she yielded to the tears that had been on the surface all day despite her companionship with Joseph and telling him everything would be fine and God would take care of him. She really believed in God's guidance and protection but it was just so very hard.

David hugged her and comforted her as she struggled to get a hold of herself and continue with the dinner everyone was so anxious to eat. It had taken all day to roast the pork and it was still slowly turning around above the fire in the fireplace. "I'll be fine. I want us all to forget our problems and to enjoy this dinner with Joseph. Get washed up and I will have it ready in about a half hour. I hope the children did not hear me."

All their grown children would be there for the dinner. Elizabeth would be coming with her husband, Augustus. Susannah missed Elizabeth helping with the dinner but she wanted her to just come for the dinner. Elizabeth was in her last months of pregnancy. She was in the stage now when she avoided leaving home to attend even family events. She felt she couldn't miss this dinner when her brother, Joseph was getting ready to travel so far away so that he could get the education he needed. Samuel had even come for the dinner, made it despite his duties with the King's Navy. Susannah felt more at ease with joining the colonies in their right to freedom from England. She believed everyone had a right to their own opinion but she didn't know why Nova Scotia had never gone through with acknowledging they were the fourteenth colony. Of course Samuel's sympathy was with England and he was glad to be part of the King's Navy.

Susannah didn't know why he had thought it was necessary to wear his uniform today. Henry was coming from the Orchard to see Joseph off also. Susannah didn't know how David would get along without Henry's help. She knew David would expect Henry to go on to school also when he was old enough. Susannah welcomed Anne and Sarah home from the orchard also. They had worked so hard in the orchard but they were willing helpers doing all they could to make this meal special. Ann had made the apple cobbler dessert before she left this morning to help with the apple picking. Hannah and Susie were still playing in the leaves out in the yard so Elizabeth went out to bring them in for the dinner. Baby Daniel was still in his cradle taking a nap. The house was abuzz with all the family activity and Susannah was pleased that their whole family was here together to see Joseph off.

It wasn't long until everyone was around the table. David had made this table years ago so that all their children could sit down with them for their dinners. David carved the pork roast while Susannah dished out the sauerkraut with all the ingredients she put in….the apples, onions grated potatoes and a little bit of sugar and salt to bring out the flavor of this dish. The cottage cheese fritters were hot and ready to eat. She knew everyone would appreciate Joseph's favorite dinner.

David sat at the head of the table with Susannah at the foot. Elizabeth and Augustus sat beside Susannah with Samuel and Henry beside David. John was next, sitting beside Anne and Sarah. Joseph was across from them with Hannah, Susannah, David and William on

4

that side. James sat across from them. Susannah and David were so proud of their children. God had blessed them with a beautiful family.

As they would enter their Congregational Church, Susannah would never forget to praise God for their beautiful family. They had their family pew and would all sit together every Sunday.

The table conversation was quiet at first and then it seemed like everyone was talking at once. They were all wondering what the sloop would look like. Joseph would be boarding soon. "I hope there are no pirates in the area," Susannah said as she finally settled down to this delicious meal.

David knew there was reason to worry about the safety of this trip for Joseph but he was determined that he would have a chance to complete his education. "I know the Captain of this sloop and I am confident he would not take a chance of docking here to pick Joseph up unless he had searched the area for pirates, Susannah." He looked at the family knowing he would not knowingly put any of them in danger. He enjoyed working with each one that helped in the apple orchard. Joseph was the fourth son and he knew all his sons would not be able to make their living on their orchards. Samuel had chosen the English Navy and was adamant about his loyalty to England.

As Joseph talked about getting George Washington to help them with the Sons of Liberty and to obtain the arms they needed Samuel hoped that there would be no trouble with the English Navy. He wasn't on duty now and he hoped that Joseph would not get involved so that they would have to face each other on different sides. He didn't want Mother worried so he didn't express his views about this. Henry seemed most interested in the orchards and was a full time partner with his father. He was right out there with the apple pickers and seeing that everything was done according to their expectations.

John was involved more into the shipping of the apples but he did go out to help in the orchards when he was needed. Anne inherited her mother's beautiful black hair and right now it was down to her waist. She tied it back when she went out to the orchard but Henry always told her to remain on the ground as she picked. She knew that was just one of the disadvantages of being a girl. She did like to help her mother in the kitchen and loved to make the desserts. She kept so active between helping with the chores and watching the children that she never gained weight from eating her share of the desserts. It was soon time to serve the apple cobbler. Susannah gave her daughter, Anne the privilege of serving the dessert since she was the one who had made it. The younger children could not wait until it was their turn to serve the dessert. David and Susannah never had any problem getting the children to do all the different chores around the house and the barn.

Everyone was anxious to contribute to the family. David and Susannah had made a game of everyone contributing to the happiness of their family. Anne would not receive points for her service. At her age of 19 she was past those kinds of games but it had given her the right habits which she never forgot. The points would be added up at the end of the month and they would receive a reward whoever had points that outnumbered the other children.

"Mother," William said, "My piece is not as big as everyone else has." Even though William was only 6 years old he was very observant of the servings of dessert. He was always anxious for sweets. His eyes were filling with tears. Hannah felt sorry for him. She was only 15 but she enjoyed taking care of him and had taught him a lot of things. She thought he was so cute with his freckles and red hair. Mother put him in her charge frequently. "Will, stop crying," Hannah said. "You can have mine. We will be having apple desserts from now until the end of the season."

William wiped away his tears and gratefully exchanged desserts with her. Susannah was proud of her children for solving their problems without her assistance. She knew that Joseph would go to Connecticut with the foundation of the upbringing she and David were trying to teach all the children. Joseph was feeling grief thinking of leaving his family for this trip.

He looked at his father. David was just finishing his dessert. "Papa, do you think I could come back for the summer and be here for the farming and caring for the orchard? I know Henry and John are here to help but you could always use another hand."

David glanced at Susannah as he pondered his question. He knew it would be hard to get him out of the country safely and it would involve the same thing to bring him back again for the summer but still it could get better and all this war talk stop. "We will see how the war situation comes along and how we could manage to get you home, son."

This was so hard on David sending his son on to school but he knew Joseph had the love of learning and knowledge he needed to succeed. He was only 17 and throughout the winter months had read the law books his Uncle Samuel had left there when he was visiting them a few years ago.

Davy was 9 years old and feeling a lot older than his brother, William. He shared a room with James and William. He looked up at his mother and thought it was time to let her know he was too old to share a room with two little brothers. His brown eyes sparkled as he looked at his mother. "I have an idea, Mother. With Joseph leaving we will have an extra bedroom. I always liked his room in the attic. Could I have his room? Just think we will have more room around this table too." Mother looked at him with tears in her eyes. She had to leave the table or she would be crying in front of everyone.

David sighed as his wife quickly left the table. "Let's take care of all this when Joseph leaves, Davy. Your mother loves each one of you so much she feels blue when anyone of you leave. I'm sure she will be right back so just finish your meal." There was a moment of quietness and then the noise of the pewter ware as each of them finished their dessert. David sent Sarah for the Bible and then some of them had presents to give to Joseph.

Susannah came back to the table with a quilt over her arm. Her eyes were still glistening with tears. "I am giving this Martha Washington Quilt to you, Joseph. I hope it will not be too hard to transport on the sloop. I understand your interest in the colonies wish to have their own government. I also understand other people wanting to stay neutral or even wanting to stay with their home country of England. Our church is staying neutral. Joseph, in going to Connecticut and talking to our relatives there you might be able to make an intelligent decision. You might be able to understand why George Washington could not help your group to join in the fight for freedom. We will be looking for letters from you. I am sure they will get through by the ships that dock here. Martha Washington does her part in joining with the ladies around about her to help the soldiers with their clothing needs. This is made from her star block pattern. You know, Joseph you and all of you," she said looking around at each one at the table," are stars to me. Each one of you has a special place in my heart."

David came to her side and putting his arm around Susannah said, "We both love all of you and you know how much we love our Lord. We know he will take care of you, Joseph. For our scripture this day we will leave you with these verses. 'Thy word is a lamp unto my feet, and a light unto my path.' Psalms 119:105 and Psalms 32:8, 'I will instruct thee and teach thee in the way which thou shalt go: I will guide thee with mine eye.' And we don't wish to forget this one. 'The steps of a good man are ordered by the Lord: and he delighteth in his way' from Psalms 37:23." Everyone joined hands as David prayed for Joseph as he would make this journey.

It wasn't a long way to the dock but only two of them would go with Joseph. David chose Henry and John to accompany them. Joseph knew all his brothers and sisters wanted to go along but David thought there would be too much commotion if they all went.

Just as it was getting dark everyone gathered around Joseph and wished him well on his journey. Joseph held baby Daniel while shaking hands and hugging each of his brothers and sisters. He knew Daniel would probably be walking when he next saw him.

Babies changed so fast. "Please pray for me….all of you. I will try my best to do well with my studies and to make you all proud of me. I will think about you all and pray for you. I know that God will watch over me and you also while we are absent one from another. God bless you all," he said as he handed Daniel over to his mother. He turned and walked away with his father, David, and his brothers, Henry and John.

The wagon was outside the gate with all his possessions he was taking with him. Their two work- horses were hitched to the wagon. Mars and Star were always faithful. They were more than ready to start on this trip. Joseph reached into the wagon to get his extra coat as the night air was chilly this time of year. He hoped that the possessions he was taking would fit into the space he would have on the sloop. David was sitting on the wagon seat with the reins in his hands.

"I think there is room up here, Joseph. No need to climb into the wagon. Now, remember we must be very still when we approach the dock. You never know who might be hiding in the woods alongside the river or who might be following the sloop. We must be very careful. You fellows are very intelligent and know you don't need to cause any problems. I will tell you when the coast is clear." David prepared to give the horses the signal they needed to proceed. It was quiet as they proceeded to the dock with the only noise being the horses' hoofs as they carried their passengers along.

John had a hard time keeping still. There was so much he wanted to tell Joseph but with all the family talking at their dinner he couldn't get a word in edgewise. He thought there would be time for more conversation once they reached their destination. He would miss Joseph. Henry didn't have as many friends as his brother, John. He was so involved in the partnership with his father and took care of all the paper work besides working in the fields and in the orchards. John was busy selling their produce and had made many friends through his work. John intended to be married soon to Mary and all the family was happy about the marriage. Mother wanted John to wait until he was twenty one and they had agreed to that. Mary would fit right into the family. Their families had been friends for a long time. Mary and John caused a lot of comment when seen together. They were a pleasant picture with Mary and her blond hair and John so tall, dark and handsome with his black hair. They could see in the distance at last the sloop docked at shore. It looked like the topmast was damaged. They were wondering what could have happened as David pulled the wagon up and tied the reins to a hitching post. Mars and Starr seemed ready to rest from the journey. The white flag was flying. David knew they must have run into some pirates. David approached the sloop as he motioned to his sons to stay back until he could find out the circumstances of the sloop. His friend, Bob came out of the woods. "I've been waiting for your arrival, Dave. I didn't want to make any more commotion than necessary. As you can see from here, we had to deal with some pirates. I guess you can see our topmast is damaged. We will fix that tonight and should be on our way again before dawn. The pirates tried to stop us and even were in the process of boarding our ship. They didn't know we had a crew that knew how to fight and fight they did. Half of them landed in the ocean and I don't know how many died or how many are planning to stop us again but we are prepared." Bob was out of breath by the time he had talked to David.

"Do you think our son will be safe if we sent him with you now?" David said with a worried look. "Two of our other sons are along with us to see him off. We will be quiet about all this and send him if you think it will work. These are perilous times we are living in I guess."

"David, we will have to learn to live with this. Some of the countries are even hiring privateers to benefit their country and to see that we don't win this war. I better get back to the sloop and we will get your son on board. You know I will take care of him as I would my own son, David. I am sure God is with us and we will overcome. We have weapons on board and everything we would need to defend ourselves. You know word goes around and I am sure the other pirates have heard about the conquest of their comrades. The mast will be finished in no time. Joseph and I will be able to carry his things to the ship. We will go through the woods. Joseph can tell his brothers goodbye here and we will be on our way."

"I trust your decision, Bob. I trust God to take care of him and know he will land in Connecticut with no problem. I will get Joseph to meet you here with his baggage." David shook Bob's hand and joined his sons. He walked silently to where his sons waited. He quickly explained the situation to them and Joseph bid his brothers goodbye. David and Joseph carried the baggage that Joseph wanted to bring with him and met Bob at the edge of the forest. David handed his part of the baggage to Bob and quickly turned to proceed into the woods and to the sloop. David's head was down as he went back to the wagon. He hoped and prayed that he had made the right decision.

CHAPTER 2
Rumors of War

JOHN WAS STANDING BESIDE the horses when David came back. Henry was staying in the woods keeping in hiding from any pirates lurking nearby. David could still see the top of the mast and realized it had been repaired. Henry came running back to them from the woods. "I saw Joseph get into the sloop." Henry was all out of breath as he was talking. "I went into the woods as far as possible and there…I think you can see the sloop now also. I was worried when I saw someone come out of the woods. He was limping and dressed as I imagine pirates dress. I could see he had a couple pistols and a cutlass on his belt. He ran but couldn't get to the sloop in time. He shot at them but they didn't stop."

"I guess that is the noise we heard while standing here," David said. "and it wasn't until we heard the noise of the gun that I was aware we have another passenger." Luci stood with her head down, crying quietly. Her best friend was gone to Connecticut. "I suppose you both knew all about her. I don't know how you kept her hidden." David could not help but be in sympathy with Luci. Everyone knew she was a good dog and faithful to all of them but especially to Joseph. Her yellow coat shown in the moonlight.

"She was with me all the time in the back of the wagon, Papa," John said, "Joseph had already bid her good-bye while you were looking for your friend. You are easily fooled anyway. Remember how long it took you a few years ago to realize that Sarah had a rabbit in the house? We didn't plan to take Luci with us. She just came when you were getting the horses hitched to the wagon. We told her to be quiet and as usual she obeyed orders. Now the whole family has bid Joseph goodbye."

"The man with Joseph was a friend of mine. I met him at church when we were growing up. His whole family went to the same church as we attend now. I know he will protect Joseph at all costs. I don't entirely agree with what he is doing right now. I know he is in the trade business but at the same time I think he co-operates with the privateers that he knows. I know that God will take care of Joseph and he will arrive safely to Connecticut. Let's go home and tell your mother that Joseph is on the sloop and on his way to Uncle John's. He will feel right at home there. They have a large family." You could hear the roar of the ocean in the background as they left the area.

John took charge of the reins and David collapsed in the back of the wagon while Henry sat with John. It wasn't a long way home but by the time they arrived it was midnight. The children had gone to bed but Susannah was still up and waiting for them.

Henry and John said they were tired and headed for bed. Susannah ran to David and into his arms. "He is fine, dear. Bob met us in the woods and we could see that they reached the sloop. I know all is well. Bob will probably be coming back near here when he returns to Nova Scotia and I know if he has any news he will come and tell us all about it. Did you know Luci was with us? I didn't know it until we heard some gun shots. I didn't mean to worry you. It didn't prevent Bob and Joseph to board the sloop. Everything is fine and all the family bid good-bye to Joseph, even Luci."

Susannah was calming down but still was wishing that Joseph could have stayed at home. She couldn't find a handkerchief to wipe away her tears and David gently wiped them away for her. "Bob wouldn't let us come all the way down to the sloop. He had some trouble with pirates and was in the process of fixing the damage they had done when they had jumped his sloop. We could see Joseph board the sloop from the edge of the forest. We know he was able to bring all his baggage on with him." David didn't tell her about the pirate they saw trying to board the sloop. It was enough that he told her inadvertently about the gun shot they heard. He thought he would tell her about the attempted pirate boarding another time.

"It's time for us to go to bed, dear." David escorted her to their bedroom and Susannah calmed down as she removed her apron and dress. David helped her with all the buttons down the back of the dress. Susannah's hands were shaking as she took her petticoat off and donned her nightgown. Silently Susannah asked God to give her strength and let her face this in a Christian way. She trusted God to take care of her whole family. By the time Susannah was ready for bed David was going to sleep.

Susannah whispered goodnight and settled down to go to sleep herself. They awakened to the sound of the children getting up to do their chores.

Daniel was crying in his cradle ready to be fed. Young David passed the bedroom all dressed to take care of some of the milking. He was such a faithful nine year old boy. Susannah nursed baby Daniel and joined them in starting the day. Her dear husband was right behind her. He was proud of his son getting the milking started without his help.

Hannah and Susie went out to gather the eggs while Sarah helped her mother with the breakfast. Hannah mixed up the pancakes while Susannah put the bacon on to cook. Daniel was sitting in his high chair his Papa had made for him. He was biting on the hard crust his mother had given him. He was teething and liked to bite on something hard while waiting for his breakfast. Everyone wondered about the cooperation in this family. David and Susannah would say that it was the way God led them with raising their family and that they all made a game of the tasks that were accomplished. The afternoon was always set aside for studies. Susannah and David always made time for their recess in the afternoon except for the time when they were needed in the orchard.

They all sat down at the table together every day for their dinner hour and talked over the events of the day. William and James kept them laughing at their perspective of their accomplishment in the apple orchard. They recounted one mealtime how William lost James who he was supposed to look after as they rescued the apples that fell on the ground. William, with his six-year-old wisdom told how four-year-old James tried to hide from him in a pile of leaves but "I saw James' foot sticking out and he could hardly keep from laughing, Mother," he said and just the way he recounted the event everyone was laughing around the table.

Hannah had noted for her mother's benefit, "Don't worry, Mother. I could see everything even though I am not allowed to go up on the ladder. Remember, I am fifteen now and I keep them both in my eyesight."

Everyone left the table and continued with the chores so that they could get out to the orchard and continue picking the apples. Susannah and the girls would be preparing apples for drying and dreaming of the nice desserts they would have for the winter when they would put the dried apples in apple cobbler, pies and other dishes that they liked.

Susannah knew this was an important part of her daughter's education. She wanted them to be ready for marriage and for homemaking when they reached that age. They didn't study in the afternoon when there was work on the farm or in the orchards.

Susannah tutored them with the help of David, especially with their Bible studies in the evening. After their day of working they all enjoyed the delicious evening meal their mother had prepared for them. "I am glad you all had a good time. If you are all finished we need to clear the table and have our Bible studies first. It will be time soon to light the candles and you know it is much easier to study with the daylight still coming into the house. Anne, I know you are tired helping me with the washing all day long but if you and Sarah would clear the table I will get everything ready for our studies. Mammy even came out of her cabin to help with the washing. I persuaded her to go back and rest.

She helped with Daniel yesterday and that is all I expect her to do today. She has always been so good with the children. She has been such a blessing to us, David."

"I know she has been a jewel, Susannah. She gave up so much to stay with us when the slaves were freed. It was Papa's wish that they all be freed at his death and we tried to carry out his wishes but Mammy would not budge. I know she was devastated to see Joseph leave yesterday. She couldn't bear to tell him goodbye yesterday. I know Joseph understood."

Mother proceeded to gather up the horn-books and they did have a few primers that just came out for the children to learn. They knew children were not ready to learn very much until the age of 7 but William and James were working on learning their alphabet. Anne and Sarah were giggling and talking about going this Saturday evening on a hayride with the young people from church. The dishes were soon taken care of and the room was quiet with all the pewterware put away once again. Hannah and Susie knew it would be their turn next. In fact Mother and Papa had given them permission to go for the hay ride this Saturday. Susie would be 13 years old soon and Hannah was already 15. David had his Bible ready and Susannah brought the others to the table. They believed that the Bible was the end and means of education. David made sure they all had their own bibles by the time they could read. They all found their places at the table as Papa prepared to lead them in their devotions. They would get through the Bible in a year.

"Let us all turn to Amos 1." Papa said. "We should all find something interesting in the book of Amos and something we can learn to help us through our life. Amos was a farmer just like we are here. In my travels I have seen the immorality of our neighboring countries. God is not pleased with them and is punishing them for their sins. God expects us to live our faith as we carry on our daily work. He expects us to be honest and show integrity in our daily living. Now do we all have the portion of scripture we are to read today?"

Anne and Sarah were helping William and James find the place in the Bible. James had just received his new Bible for Christmas and he was starting to recognize some of the letters in the alphabet that were written down on his hornbook. He wanted to know as much about the alphabet as his brother, William. Papa could see everyone was ready to read their portion of the scripture. "Davy, you can start reading and go around the circle with a couple verses for each. Anne and Sarah will help you, William and James." David was very patient and listened as each one read their portion.

David was so proud of his family and praised God for the blessing of having such a large family. David closed in prayer and Susannah proceeded in helping the children in their lessons for the day. It wasn't long until they were all done and ready for Susannah's inspection.

The candles were lit and the hornbooks put away along with the pages of penmanship Hannah and Susie had completed. "I wonder when we will receive a letter from Joseph." Hannah asked. Mother looked up from her task of correcting the papers.

"I wonder every day when a letter will come," she said as she looked to David for an answer. "It couldn't come for at least a week, Susannah.

I know they will land safely and we will hear soon. I believe it is time for us all to go to bed. It has been a very busy day for all of us. We will pray the Lord's Prayer tomorrow. It is on the back side of your horn books, William and James."

Everyone except David and Susannah, and their oldest children were in bed. Samuel was always in their prayers. He had chosen to serve with the Navy of England and they were not too pleased with his decision. However, they stood for freedom of choice and would not ever stand in his way. They didn't like the idea that he might not choose ever to live in Nova Scotia. Right now he was interested in a girl living in Scotland. He tended to favor his mother's family with his black hair and beautiful blue eyes. Then there was Henry who was a valued partner in their farming which included all their orchards. He stood out in the community with his red hair and efficiency. Next there was Elizabeth who was already married to Augustus Willoughby and expecting their first grandchild. They had a lovely home near them on a portion of the land David had given them for a wedding present. Then there was John who was interested in Mary from their church but he was only 20 years old and David thought he should wait until he was 21 for marriage.

He was very tall with black hair and so talkative that he was already helping with the services at church. At 19 and 18 years old, Anne and Sarah were asking to go to all the functions of the church where young people were involved. Susannah especially prayed for them. They would all miss Joseph and wondered now if he had arrived safe to his destination. They hoped he would take advantage of the education he was now to be involved with and use it to become a successful lawyer as his Uncle Samuel in Connecticut who had just been appointed to serve in Congress. David hoped that Joseph would follow their church in staying neutral through this problem with England. He still hoped that disagreement would not end in a war. He would lose no time in calling Joseph home if that would happen. Their daughter Hannah was 15 and starting to want to go on the hay rides and join the young people in their activities. They knew if they let Hannah go then it wouldn't be long until Susan would want to join her and she was only 13. David, William and James were all in bed now. Baby Daniel had been nursed and put to bed before their prayer time. They knew all their children were under God's care and that God remembered all their names. They could go to bed knowing that God cared for each one of them.

Weeks went by before the promised letter was delivered to the Starr family. David was the first to see his friend coming up the lane on his horse, Victory. David knew he must have news of Joseph and he ran down the lane to meet him. Bob stopped to talk to David.

"I have good news, David. Let me get Victory settled and then I will give you the letter Joseph wrote to you. He looks good. Nothing to worry about." Bob rode the horse to the hitching post and dismounted to talk to the family. Susannah was already out in the yard to meet him and the children were right behind her except for Daniel who was down for his afternoon nap. David was out of breath when he ran up to the yard. "Come in, Bob. I know Susannah still has the dinner out. She was just clearing everything off the table when I thought I heard someone approaching on a horse and ran out to greet you."

"I'll be glad to have something to eat….especially some of your cooking, Susannah. Let's all go in and I will give you the letter and report what I know about his situation." Bob looked forward to a good homemade meal. He always saw that his comrades had enough food but with the equipment they had on the sloop it wasn't always the most appetizing meal. "First I will say that I went to see Joseph at the Starr home and found him happy and looking good. He said he enjoyed his studies and was going to church with his Aunt and Uncle. I am not sure but their daughter, Joanna seemed to be listening with rapture to his every word with me. She is a beautiful young girl. She had prepared a lot of the meal I had there. They have a really nice family and they seemed to all cooperate together just as yours does, David."

Bob handed the letter to David and sat down to eat in the seat Susannah indicated. David sat down across from him and opened the letter. "I will just read through this quickly and then read it out loud for everyone to hear," David said. He frowned and stopped as he read the first words. "William, run out to Mammy's cabin and tell her we received a letter from Joseph. I know she will want to hear this letter read." William immediately ran out to tell Mammy the good news. Even he knew how much Mammy missed Joseph.

October 19, 1775
Dear Mother and Papa;

I am glad Bob can deliver this letter to you. It has been exciting here. I was surprised to see they had a group of 'Sons of Liberty". I wanted to join but Uncle John said I should wait for your permission before I did that. We had an exciting time coming over here. A group of pirates tried to board our ship. Your friend is very good in leading his men to just the right approach in order to get by them. He can tell you better than I can all about our experiences with them. I feel right at home here with Uncle John and his family. I couldn't have a better Auntie who is so sweet and tries to help me with my studies and provides a special place so that I can study in peace. Of course, I am at home with a large family around me. I couldn't join George Washington's army in Nova Scotia but I could here. In fact, I witnessed a group who were ready to sign up in the town. I had met Joseph Plumb Martin and at only 15 he was one of the first to sign up. I don't know how far this revolution will go but they all seemed determined to fight for freedom. I heard that Martin's grandparents where he was living were against it but they helped him get ready. All you needed was some socks, a pair of shoes, a couple knickers and shirts. It sounded good to me. I hope Nova Scotia joins in. Hope everyone is well.

Your son, Joseph

David was livid with rage. Susannah had never seen him so angry and was worried about where this would lead them. David struggled to control himself in front of his friend and his family. "I'll not stand for this," he said as he handed the letter to Susannah and went out to the yard to simmer down.

Susannah prepared to read the letter to the family. Everyone was sitting on the edge of their chairs wondering what had made Papa so angry with Joseph. He was always so proud of Joseph...in fact with all his children....and especially in front of his friends. This was all out of character for David. They had never seen Papa so out of control. Susannah waited until William came back with Mammy to hear the letter.

Bob listened with the family as Susannah read the letter. Bob knew David was against getting into the conflict of the Revolution. He was not getting involved and did not want anyone in his family join forces with the Patriots. David was neutral and joining with their church in announcing their neutral stand. They had even written to the government of England that they desired to remain neutral and would appreciate it if they were not required to take part in this war at all. They added that this is the only way they could live safely in their homes. Bob was just contented to make money with his trade business. It was a problem dealing with the pirates so he might change his mind and stop his trading until after this conflict was over. Bob saw David coming up the path to join the family once again.

The house was quiet when David entered the doorway. Susannah was cutting the cake for their dessert. She looked at David with compassion. She knew that he was regretting his decision to send Joseph to Connecticut for his studies. She hoped that everything would work out and their son could come back home.

"Sorry about that, Bob. Our son is so young and it seems to him an exciting thing to do joining up with the patriots. I know he wanted George Washington to help his group to obtain arms and join in the fight. I thought some time it might come to a Revolution but I didn't know it would come so fast."

Soon everyone was enjoying the delicious cake Susannah served. Bob had really enjoyed the home-cooked meal. It was a great change from eating the food prepared on board ship. "I understand how you feel, David. It is hard to let our children grow up and make their own decisions. I hope there is a solution to your problem. I know we both believe in prayer so I will remember to pray for Joseph. Thank you for this delicious dessert, Susannah. I'll always know where to stop in for a delicious meal."

Bob retrieved his jacket in preparation for leaving this family. "Did you want me to wait for a reply to the letter, David? I will be stopping by in a week so if you want to wait until then I will be sure to stop in to pick it up."

"I think Susannah will want to have some part in this letter and also the children so I would appreciate you stopping by again. Thanks so much for bringing his letter to us, Bob."

Bob continued to put on his jacket and prepare to leave. David had fed Bob's horse when he went out so abruptly. He was quickly on his way to his own home. His home was closer to the Cornwallis River. He wondered as he left his friend what kind of letter David would write to his son. He had enjoyed taking him to Connecticut and even met the family where Joseph would be staying. He didn't think Joseph would ever make Connecticut his home. He wondered as he looked at the scenery around him how anyone ever could leave this beautiful country with the ocean nearby and all the hills and mountains around them. He knew David wanted Joseph to get the education that Uncle Samuel had and he hoped David's dreams for his son would come true. Time would tell how everything would turn out.

CHAPTER 3
Choosing Sides

MAMMY WAS NOT EXPECTED to get up early in the morning anymore. Her duties were a lot less with baby Daniel than they were with the other children. She had enjoyed taking care of all the children and was heartbroken when Joseph was sent off to college in Connecticut. She always enjoyed her conversation with Joseph and treated him as she would her own grandson. She always made sure she had cookies baked when he appeared at her cabin door. She enjoyed the other children as well and never regretted staying with this family instead of taking her freedom as the other slaves had.

She was so glad to see Samuel when he came home to see Joseph before he headed off to school. Samuel was telling her about the girl he met in Scotland and how he was trying to get time off from the English Navy to bring her back to meet his family.

It was critical to him that his family would like Emily. Mammy smiled as she thought of him and his growing up days. He always acted like he was in charge of all the children. He took his place as the oldest in the family seriously and really felt responsible for all the children. Samuel grew up to be such a handsome young man with his height and his black hair. She knew Mr. David and Miss Susannah were very proud of him even though they weren't happy with his choice of fighting for England.

His brother, Henry, was so entirely different. Henry would rather stay home and had no interest in serving in any military branch. He remained neutral and would keep on working on the farm and orchards. He was a good partner to his father and she understood his parents' love and pride when they talked about Henry. Henry took after a grandfather from England with his stocky build and his red hair. Mammy thought back to his boyhood and cherished all the input she had in his upbringing - his kindness and love for his family...the way he cooperated with his brothers. She knew he would do everything possible to be a good representative to the community and with his business endeavors to help his brother, John.

Mammy was looking forward to holding yet another baby before God's time to take her to heaven. Elizabeth would soon have her baby. Mammy could remember the times Elizabeth would come over to the cabin to play with her dolls. She especially liked the one Mammy had made her. Mammy knew that someday she would be a good mother. Everyone liked her husband, Augustus, also. Mammy knew he would be a good father to the baby. Elizabeth looked a picture of her mother with her black hair and blue eyes.

She couldn't believe that John was 20 years old now. Elizabeth had been only one year old when her brother, John was born. It was like taking care of twins. Mammy was so glad she was there to help Miss Susannah. She had a good time taking care of all of the children but John was so talkative even before his third birthday. He was good now at his job as a merchant but Mammy knew he would also make a good Pastor. He had the understanding and interest in the people around him that you see in Pastors. His testimony touches everyone's heart that hears him.

Mammy leaned back in her rocker as she thought about her sweet girls, Anne and Sarah. Anne was doing so well with her cooking abilities and Sarah was gifted with the ability to stitch beautiful samplers. Anne had the same coloring as her mother with her black hair and blue eyes while Sarah was so pretty with her auburn hair and quiet spirit.

She was in her own world as she proceeded with her newest project in a secluded place she would find in the house. Everyone admired her fancy work. Mammy loved it when she would decide to spend some time with her while she embroidered her tiny stitches.

How often Mammy wished they could just all gather round about her as she told them stories of bygone days…stories of her childhood and the different things that happened to them when their father was growing up. How he always stood up for them and would never want them to be disciplined for thoughtless behavior. How they all felt when their grandfather had passed on and they were all liberated. Mammy felt so close to the whole family she just could not bring herself to leave them. Hannah was fifteen now as Joseph was going off to school. Hannah was a good helper to her mother and helped with the harvesting of the apples and blueberries. She was a very pretty young girl and she never forgot to look Mammy up every morning with her beautiful smile and happy outlook on life.

Susannah, named after her mother, was all of thirteen years old now and tended to be a tomboy running around after David who was nine years old. David was cute with his brown eyes that sparkled with mischief. Mammy gave him a hug whenever he ran past her. He definitely needed the baskets with the false bottom for picking the apples. He was caught lots of times playing instead of helping with the chores. She couldn't count the times she had to sew up his breeches again.

William was only six years old and enjoyed being a part of this family. He had freckles and red hair. He loved running after Luci, the golden Labrador and chasing after the black kitten too.

James was his constant companion at the age of four. Mammy loved looking after them although she could not keep up with them. They enjoyed coming into her cabin and listening to Mammy's stories. When she told them her dog stories they could almost see the dogs running after a ball and their ears bouncing up and down. Everyone loved Mammy and she knew their steps before they ever entered the door.

Mammy didn't see baby Daniel as much as she saw the others through their babyhood. Susannah thought it was too much for her to watch him very often and then he was at an age where he needed his mother's care. Mammy knew she could help her better in other ways.

Mammy still remembered when Susannah and David were married. She was overjoyed David found a beautiful girl with so much faith in God. She was so glad she was appointed to be Susannah's personal maid. It wasn't long until she was serving Susannah as a freed slave. It was good to have her freedom but she wanted to use her freedom to work for Mr. David. She still saw the other people from the plantation because they stayed in the area and worked for David. A lot of them were able to build their own houses and live in the community. Others had gone back to help fight in this Revolutionary War. In fact there were whole armies of black soldiers that really helped in the war effort. It was appreciated by all the citizens in the thirteen colonies.

Mammy rocked back in her rocker as she considered all these events that happened since Miss Susannah came here right after their marriage. She knew they were answering a letter they had received from Joseph. She thought they might call her in to add to it but so far she had not received an invitation. She knew they would tell her all about it later. She had plenty of darning and patching to do for them until they needed her for something else. Davy and William were especially hard on their clothing. She had several pairs of knickers to patch and socks to darn. She had just darned another pair of socks when she heard someone at the door. It sounded like William.

"Mammy, Mother wants you to come to the house!" he called to her. "Just a minute, William….I will get there soon as my rheumatism lets me, child." She could hear him say, "Don't know how Mammy knows I am here without opening her door. Must have special eyes," he muttered as he headed back home. She followed him to the house and found everyone still around the table. This was truly her family and when they were happy she was happy, when they were hurt, she hurt. The Starr family had been her family her whole life.

"I was wondering where everyone was this afternoon. Thought you all might be studying but then I heard that your friend had come to spend some time with you so thought I would stay out of the way, Mr. David."

"Mammy, we wanted you to help us answer this letter from Joseph and before we answered it we wondered if you had a message for him also. Bob is stopping by on his way back," he said as he pulled a chair out for Mammy to sit down with them. It always amazed Mammy to be treated so respectfully by the whole family. There were still families that had slaves brought over from Connecticut who were not treated as well as she had always been even before her release from slavery. She knew that God had truly blessed this family.

"I really miss that boy, Mr. David. He reminds me of your growing up days. I hopes you will always be proud of him. I know he didn't want to go away to school but yet he respected you and your decision about him."

Susannah held up the letter. "David is very concerned about him now, Mammy. We already read the letter and he is very concerned about what Joseph plans. I will read it to you again and maybe you can give us some advice about it." Susannah opened the letter and proceeded to read it aloud.

Mammy listened intently and knew right away David's problem with the letter. She leaned over and touched his arm. "Mr. David,

I know how you were angry at the letter but remember he is at an age now when even dangerous adventures seem good to him. He has wanted to join the Sons of Liberty for a long time. There aren't many free people like me. They are slaves and want their freedom so they understand the colonies fighting for just that. Just think this thing through. Could be you will change your mind."

David was still angry when she advised him. Usually she would never disagree with him. "When you write the letter, Susannah, I want you to tell him I will disinherit him if he does not immediately return. I've had enough of this talk about the Sons of Liberty. I am very committed to everyone having their liberty, Mammy, but this goes too far to turn the whole country to war in order to establish the colonies' freedom from England. England has never done anything to deserve this. In fact it will impoverish the whole country because they have just spent so much on a war with France. Samuel Willoughby, the father of Augustus has declared the raising of a regiment here would be the ruin of the place and Faith he would put a stop to it.…he would not have the people of the town so imposed upon as to be enlisted and decoyed away.…swore that he would go to Halifax and put a stop to those [!!**??!!] recruiting officers for it would ruin the town, and it should not be." Susannah looked shocked at David's language and instructed the children to go out to play. Mammy was sad at the evidence of David's temper. She thought David would someday be sorry for his remarks. She remembered his joy when he could announce his father's intention to free all his slaves after he was gone and the will was read.

"David," she said, "If you could just tell Joseph that his mammy still loves him no matter what decision he makes but it would be wise to listen to his parents as he always did. I know, David, before you make a decision about Joseph you will consult God. We know that God has a plan for each of our lives. You have both been good parents and it has been a joy to help you raise your family. We don't know what situation he is in but I pray every day that God will lead him in the right way. Thank you for asking me to add to the letter."

Tears were in her eyes as she left them to write the letter. She went back to her cabin to continue her sewing projects.

The children were still playing out in the yard and Susannah was left alone with David. "We need to think this over as Mammy said, David. We stood behind Samuel when he decided to join the British Navy and Henry when he wanted to stay neutral along with the church. We always stood for freedom, honey." David really knew Susannah was right but this Revolutionary War was causing him so much grief. Before he knew it, Samuel and Joseph would be fighting each other. That could not be. He felt the need to get Joseph back home until this war was over. He imagined living any longer in Connecticut would change Joseph into a Patriot for sure. "Let's finish the letter, Susannah," he said. "We want to have it ready when Bob comes back through here. I will try to think this through better. Did everyone get a chance to write something in the letter?"

"Let's get them all in and see if anyone has something more to add. This will be a thick letter," Susannah said. She felt David's distress but she didn't know what to do about it. She knew Joseph would have the opportunity to get better acquainted with Uncle Samuel if he hadn't already seen him. Samuel lived very close to the Starrs. She had heard that Samuel was deep into government work. She thought he was even a member of the Congress now. Samuel Huntington came from a large family and they were all devoted Christians, some of them even had become Pastors in the Congregationalist churches. Martha and Samuel were not blessed with their own children but they had adopted three children. Susannah was sure Samuel would be a good influence for Joseph.

She knew God had a plan for Joseph and she hoped they would not stand in his way. Everyone came in to add to the letter. Susannah passed it around and everyone who could write added their greetings to the letter. Anne was the first one in and wrote a whole page to Joseph. She was wondering about the church he was attending and if they had a lot of young people at that church.

She wondered about their cousins where he was living. She knew they had a daughter about the age of Joseph. Sarah wrote about her latest project she was doing with her sampler. Joseph was always interested in the items she made. He would sometimes do some interesting woodwork. Hannah was following in Sarah's steps and had made some beautiful things already. Everyone loved the rag doll she had made recently. They were wondering who would be receiving it as a Christmas gift. Probably Susie would receive it to have on her bed. She was always decorating her room with something. The boys each drew a picture of something on the farm….some of the apple trees and signed their names beneath them. The letter was soon all ready to go when Bob came by to pick it up. They all missed Joseph so very much.

Mammy was praying for them all as she was continuing with her sewing. She missed Joseph but she knew this was an opportunity for him to have a better job and to make his parents proud of him. Probably David's friend would be by for the letter tomorrow. She knew David trusted Bob to bring Joseph back if they could make arrangements for that.

Bob was there to pick up the letter the following day. David was just coming in from the orchard where they continued to pick apples and could see it coming to a close. David was pleased with the work done not only by his own family but also by the former slaves who were also his friends working in the orchards a distance from David's home.

Everything was going well which left David in a good mood today. "Good to see you, Bob," he said as he brushed off his clothes to go inside. "Come in, come in. Have a cup of coffee. Did you have your breakfast before you started out?"

Bob followed him in the house. "I had breakfast and I need to pick up your letter and get going back. I hope my sloop hasn't been bothered while I was away. We never know what can happen anymore with the pirates out there and then this war starting. My family thinks I should quit but I am not ready to do that yet. There is a lot of money to be made in trade and if I quit it affects all those working for me also. No, don't think I will quit yet. Most times the pirates will not come up close enough to harm the sloop. Good morning, Susannah."

Susannah had the letter in hand and was happy Bob was willing to deliver it. "Did you want a cup of coffee and could I serve you anything else before you continue on your journey?" she asked.

"No, this coffee will do fine. I had a large breakfast. Hope I find everything normal when I go. I heard that some of the colonies were drafting men into the army now. They didn't get enough volunteers. Don't be surprised if Connecticut has done that also."

"I swear I will disinherit Joseph if he does that, Bob. I am not going to stand by and see my sons kill each other. I want Joseph back here until this uprising has been put down and you can tell him that too."

"I will tell him just what you said, David. I don't know what the situation will be when I arrive there but I am sure Joseph will do the right thing." Bob was wondering how far Joseph would go to be able to stay there and join with the Sons of Liberty. "I think the letter is ready, David. I should start so that I can see how things are with our sloop. I know it will be a few weeks until I will be able to return." Bob bid the family good-bye and was soon on his way.

He was encountering different ideas wherever he went. How this war would come out was a mystery. Only God knew what solution was right. Everyone he met had different ideas of where to stand about this war. Some were glad that it never went through for Nova Scotia to become the 14th Colony and help fight this war.

Chapter 4
The Connecticut Continental Forces

Bob delivered the letter to the family in Connecticut. John met him at the door and immediately invited him into their home. Bob was surprised to see a long haired German Shepherd meeting him at the door. It made him feel right at home as he was accustomed to seeing Luci at the Starr home in Nova Scotia. This is the first time he met Heidi but she seemed a different kind of dog than Luci. Heidi didn't appear to be a guard dog but was friendly to everyone. As Bob was petting Heidi he turned to John.

"Good trip, John. Really surprised even me. I was surprised at the dock in Nova Scotia to find all my men there and ready to go. They had all the shipment loaded before I arrived. The men enjoyed the time off and were anxious to get started again. Everyone was talking about the news of the war situation. It is serious, John, really serious," he said as he shook hands and gave John a big hug. "Another surprise, John is to see you now have a dog here and a large one who reminds me of Luci at your brother's house in Nova Scotia." Bob continued to pet Heidi as she sat at his feet. "Doesn't seem as aggressive as Luci, though. I tell you, Luci would take you apart if she didn't know you and there was no one there to call her off. Heidi seems quieter. Where did you find her?"

"One of the families in the neighborhood had to find a new home for their dog. The husband seemed to take a disliking to her but the children were heartbroken. I told them they could come and see her as often as they wished. She has been a good dog for the children and follows everyone around. She probably would not be a good protection from strangers but I don't think she has been trained that way." John continued to welcome his friend into his home.

"Sit down, friend. I don't know how you do this work. The pirates must be out there now in full force. How are you planning to continue? You know when the colonies get a better Navy and fight England on the sea you will really be in trouble."

"I realize that, John, but I also know they need our products here and we need yours. I'll have to give it some thought. So, where is everyone? I visit David and everyone seems to be immediately at my side. I suppose I come at the wrong time."

"No, Bob. The family will soon be home. There was a fall picnic at the church. I stayed home to finish some tasks around here before the winter sets in around us. Makes me wonder how your army will survive the winter. I hear some have just walked off and gone home. I wish more people thought as our church and were neutral but then we want everyone to have the freedom they do not have with the English ruling us from across the ocean. Times are hard but I guess we will survive, Bob."

Bob noticed that John had the same physique as his brother, David. He wondered if he had the same temperament as David. "David didn't take the letter Joseph sent him too well, Bob. He was so angry he went outside to cool off. He said that in no way did he want Joseph involved in this Revolutionary War. He would even go so far as to disinherit him. I imagine that would mean that he would disown him if he even wanted to join up with the Connecticut sons of Liberty. He had nothing good to say about the recruiters. Joseph told him he saw the recruiter and so many had signed up. Joseph Plum Martin was one of the first to sign up. I know David was against George Washington helping Nova Scotia with arms or money to enlist their citizens in this war. While Joseph was so disappointed I could see David was so glad his family would not be involved in this Revolution although if he had to take sides I believe he would be all for freedom from England. He stands with his church in calling for neutrality between our countries."

The men were interrupted with the noise of the family coming back from their picnic. Joanna and Joseph came in first laughing about their good time at the picnic. You could see they enjoyed each other's company. Sarah came in next carrying baby Emma. "This is the whole family, Bob," John said as he proudly introduced each one to his friend. "They all look tired out, don't they? Too much playing, I guess but maybe it was too much good food. The young people always like it when we have these picnics at church but then the others have a great time just visiting. It will be a cold winter and then there isn't as much chance to gather all together. I seldom miss these occasions but I will make the next one. I need to keep up on my game of horseshoe there." Everyone started talking all at once about the games and contests and the food.

"Papa, you wouldn't believe who won the horseshoe game. It kind of stays in the family. Joseph won today. You should see him play." John laughed and said, "I will play a game with you here, Joseph. Ready anytime."

"I'm surprised the twins are getting so tall. How old are you, boys?" Bob asked. Bob was enjoying this family. He hadn't seen the twins when he stopped here the last time to deliver the letter.

Mark pushed Thomas up first. They were identical and always tried to confuse their relatives and friends.

They were cute little boys with freckles and red hair. "I am older than my brother, Mr. Bob," Thomas said. "I am 15 minutes older." Mark stood beside Thomas. "We will not fool you this time. We are 5 years old…..well, not until tomorrow. Mama made us a cake too."

Mark's eyes sparkled as he talked with Bob. "Are you staying for our birthday, Mr. Bob?"

"I need to get started for sure, Mark." Bob said as he kneeled down to talk to the boys. He could see that Mark was more outgoing than his twin brother. What a privilege to raise this wonderful family. It wasn't until after Thanksgiving that Bob was ready to return to Nova Scotia. He made his usual stop at the Starr home in Connecticut to pick up their letter and was on his way to the sloop in no time. He wanted to return before Christmas with his next delivery. He hoped the men were all ready to go as usual and they would not have any trouble with the pirates or the English ships. After bidding everyone goodbye he was on his way. Heidi made sure she was there at the gate to tell him goodbye. She acted like she had found a new friend. She was beautiful with her long hair and black coat. Her ears stood up in attention at all times. Her tail wagged in joy at her family coming back from the picnic. The family took her along with them at times but thought this gathering might be too many for her. She was exhausted at times playing with the children.

Joseph was having a harder time every day staying neutral. Even the fellows at the college were joining and urging him to at least join the Sons of Liberty. He kept telling them the colonies had not yet declared war and until they did he would not become involved. He didn't care who was signing up with the recruiters. He did not want to risk getting in trouble with Papa.

The Nova Scotia Starr family tried to put out thoughts of a coming war and enjoyed the holidays. They did not know what was keeping Bob but they had not seen him in months. They hoped that he was not picked up by the pirates. It sounded more and more that there would be a war. He was afraid this would be the last peaceful year of 1775. He was trying to forget about it and plan on just enjoying the holidays. It would not be long after that to plant their crops. John was already making diagrams of where each crop would be planted and do the best. It would be great to plant the fields again. He knew the horses were getting anxious to get out again in the fields.

John Walker, a family member who came to Yarmouth in 1764 from Massachusetts, was getting a petition ready on this 8th of December, 1775 for the inhabitants of Yarmouth to sign. John Walker was expressing the views of the Congregationalist Church to live in peace. The petition read, "We do all of us profess to be true friends and loyal subjects to George, our King. We were almost all of us born in New England. We have fathers, brothers and sisters in that country, divided betwixt natural affection to our nearest relations, and good Faith and Friendship to our King and Country, we want to know, if we may be permitted at this time to live in a peaceable state, as we look on that to be the only situation in which we with our wives and children, can be in any tolerable degree safe." In this document the inhabitants of Yarmouth were expressing a feeling general among Yankees in the southern section of the province.

David was perfectly willing to sign this petition. He hoped that Joseph would soon return home and avoid involvement in the Revolutionary War. He just couldn't have his sons fighting against each other. He was so glad John had put out this petition which was in the values of the Congregationalist Church where all the family attended. In fact, David was one of the members who had started the church in the first place.

As the new year rolled around it wasn't long until the recruiters were out in Connecticut to round up the men who would serve in the army. The Continental congress of 1776 had passed Eighty Eight Battalion Resolve. Each state would contribute according to population of each district. Each state was to arm, clothe and equip its regiments. They walked up to the Starr home in Connecticut and chose to recruit Joseph in the army. Joanna and Joseph were not there but her parents informed the recruiters that they didn't think Joseph was the person they were looking for. He was living with them just for the time he attended college. The recruiters declared they would be back and went on to the next person on their list.

As Joanna and Joseph came back from their walk they couldn't believe the recruiters had been there already. They had also missed the latest communication from his family in Nova Scotia. They had just received the news that Joseph was an uncle. Elizabeth and Augustus were the parents of a baby girl. Joseph was anxious to see this new member of their family but he was devastated to be torn away from Joanna also. He couldn't wait until they would be married and have their own family. He knew someway the Lord would work all this out for them. He felt the presence of the Holy Spirit and he knew that it would take all his faith to come through this time in his life.

Chapter 5
'Tis Time to Part

On June 17, 1775 the battle of Bunker Hill doused everyone's hope that something could be worked out with England. Even though it looked good at first the Patriots gave up on getting Canada involved in the conflict. There were too many people there with ties to their homeland. The King had promised rewards to anyone who would stay true to their country of England.

Christmas of 1775 passed for the patriots realizing it was time to consider separating from England. On New Year's day the British regulars in Boston sighted a curious banner flying above the American lines on Prospect Hill. They wondered if this flag could be a signal of surrender. George Washington was amused when he heard the British reaction for "we hoisted the union flag in compliment to the United Colonies." It was a flag of 13 stripes and the crossed bars of the Union Jack.

Joanna and Joseph went for a walk of this cold day in January. Joseph had declared his love for Joanna and she insisted that she would follow him wherever he would go. "I find I do not wish to go against Papa's wishes, Joanna. I would join the patriots in a minute if that was an option but you can see the problem that I find myself. Our church in Nova Scotia has asked the King to let them be neutral and I am sure he will grant that request. I would not only be going against my father's will but also against the Church's decision to remain neutral. I hear they are drafting the fellows in Connecticut and I would be the first one to sign up but I need to follow the wishes of the church." Joseph drew Johanna close to him as they walked in the cold weather. "How I love you honey, but maybe it is not only time for the colonies to part from England but for us to part until things get better. You know when I leave that I will be back for you as soon as I can." Joseph had a hard time revealing his decision to Joanna. His voice quivered as he related his decision to her. How he loved her and couldn't imagine life without her anymore. He understood a little bit his parents' devotion to each other now. Joanna's eyes were filled with tears as she answered. "I will love you forever, Joseph. I understand your decision and I hope everything will be resolved in a few months. I hope Mr. Bob is still on the sloop with his trading business but we haven't seen him for a while. However will you get back home without him to take you?" she asked. They stopped on their walk, the couple close together to brave the cold weather but also to feel each other's love and concern. "I don't know how I will get home, sweetheart but I know God knows how everything will turn out. No matter what happens, remember that we both believe God leads and guides us wherever out circumstances take us. Let us put our faith in Him."

"But what of your studies at college? That is what you came for in the first place. I know your father wants you to come home but his idea was for you to be a good lawyer, a judge sometime. He was comparing you to Samuel Huntington who has done so well as a judge and was appointed by the assembly of Connecticut to represent their colony in the Continental congress last year. You are doing so well in your college studies, Joseph that it seems terrible to throw all that away in order to return to Nova Scotia. I will back you up whatever you decide, dear because I know it is in God's hands. Oh, my, I am shivering now. We must turn around and go home," she said as she moved closer to him to not only to keep warm but to be with him as long as she could. They hurried up the steps and into the

Starr home of Connecticut only to find the recruiting officers had already been there and promised they would be back soon.

Joanna was terrified. She knew God would take care of them but everything looked so impossible. She knew Joseph had made up his mind to follow his father's wishes and wasn't about to change his mind. How could they force him to serve under a State where he was not even a citizen? Heidi seemed to know there was some kind of trouble coming. She sat by Joseph as Joanna pondered on what would happen to the love of her life. How could she be separated from him now when they had just recently found each other. Life wasn't fair but then she knew that God always had a plan for their lives. Heidi followed Joseph to the chair where he sat down to wait for the recruiters to come back. There was no use fighting this because he knew these men would not understand his wish to remain neutral in this war which he would support if he felt it was God's will for him.

It wasn't long until they heard the recruiters coming up the steps. They had a young fellow in tow that was a citizen of Connecticut but he was ready and willing to join the fight against England. He couldn't understand why Joseph did not feel the same way. The only reason he had not volunteered before was he was visiting relatives in New York at the time the recruiters came to town. He knew that John Plum Martin was one of the first volunteers. He knew Joseph from college and thought he was in favor of separating from England and establishing their own country. He was surprised to see the stand Joseph was taking to stand with his country of Nova Scotia and with his church to be neutral in this conflict. Joseph was now resisting arrest and Joanna stood by crying.

Joseph's eyes dimmed with tears as he parted from Joanna and the rest of her family. Just as he was really getting to know them he had to leave in this sad state. Joseph really wished he could join in this fight but he felt God would want him to listen to his father and to the church to make this decision. He was led along in handcuffs and wondering where they were taking him.

As he was led along Joseph could see they were heading toward the ocean. At one place they stopped to pick up some more prisoners. He turned to the recruiter leading him along. "I thought it was only volunteers that went into the army. What would George Washington say about this?" he asked.

"I guess George Washington would be surprised you did not want to join him in his fight for freedom. He has issued an order for a draft of all able bodied men to help. He didn't get enough volunteers from what I heard. Now, no more talking….keep moving. We have a ways to go yet. Do you want to change your mind and join your college friend to serve your country?"

"I wish I could join my friend but no, I am not a citizen here. We wanted to join you in Nova Scotia but George Washington said he didn't have the equipment or the funds to help us. Then when the church declared we were neutral there weren't enough men to make up an army anyway." Joseph tried to peer into the distance to see the ocean and to see if Mr. Bob's ship would be seen on the horizon. He couldn't see anything that would help him out of this situation. They had walked for about an hour and he could see that the recruiter was losing his patience. Joseph had heard someone calling the recruiter Bill. He couldn't think of anyone else he knew with as much determination to carry out the law to the fullest extent. Bill was a big man who looked like he had experience seeing justice done.

Bill turned to the procession and raising his voice so that everyone could hear, he said, "You all realize, those of you who have decided to avoid the draft that you are traitors…traitors are usually hung so you should be thankful you are not hanging on that tree yonder… in fact that sounds like a good idea to me…we have a ways to walk yet and I would just as soon end it right now. Maybe you would like to change your mind Joseph Starr...not too late yet."

Joseph looked to the Lord from whence cometh his help. He was doing this to please his father and his church. He knew God was pleased when he honored his father's wishes. He could see now there were not any sloops at the shore of the ocean so Mr. Bob was nowhere in sight. "I will stand by my decision, Sir. Is there a way I can get word to my family here in Connecticut where I will be held prisoner?"

Bill laughed so hard he nearly fell down as he was walking. "We will send a messenger right out to tell them, Joseph. You know we don't do that but you better hope they find out where you are or you might starve. Someone will have to bring you food and if anyone brings you something you will probably be fighting to get your share. There are more prisoners where you are going and you will find they are a sight. I hear there is a whole crew of a sloop picked up for piracy. They are a rough group of men. Now, no more talking...we have to walk along the shore here where it is rough."

The men continued to walk, some almost falling to the ocean, so tired they felt like they could not go another step. It didn't sound like they would be any better off when they arrived at their destination. It was very windy walking by the ocean and so cold, coldest he had felt since he left Nova Scotia. Some of the prisoners did not have any warm clothing at all. Joseph at least had a coat. He thought how distressed Joanna and her whole family would be about him. He couldn't understand why John was forced to march with them to the prison when he had told them he would join the army. Maybe he could communicate to him to try to let Joanna know where he was held. He would look for a chance to do that. Some of the men were falling down from exhaustion but were quickly prodded up to continue on their journey to their jail. They eventually came to an abandoned ware-house with bars on the few windows. Joseph knew immediately this must be the place where they would be held. As Bill opened the door he could smell the stench he would be living in for no telling how long. He said a word of prayer as he entered this unimaginable place. He had never seen men so thin or in such a state of hunger and with torn clothing as these men were. Some were laying on ragged blankets moaning in pain with no help available. Joseph knew there was a Congregationalist Church near here and if they knew of the conditions these men were in he was sure they would find a way to help them. He needed to get word to John. He noticed Bill talking to the man in charge here and John standing nearby so he approached them.

"I thought this would change your mind, Joseph. If this doesn't, nothing will change it for sure," Bill said laughing.

"No, Sir. I just wanted to bid John goodbye. I wish I was in his shoes and could join him in the fight for liberty but I am not free to do that."

Bill turned to the jailer then, disgusted with Joseph and his decision. This gave Joseph a few minutes to talk to John. "John, could you notify the Congregationalist Church about this prison? I know it is near here and maybe they will help some." The man in charge pulled them in and shut the door.

"I will do my best," John whispered as Bill turned to usher him out of there. He turned the prisoners over to the man in charge as he left. Bill noticed the guard - house as he left. He thought this must be how this man could stand his turn guarding these prisoners. He evidently spent most of his time outside the prison house and went to the guard- house to guard the prison.

"All of you new ones listen up….you can call me Mr. Brooks or just Sir". I will not stand for any complaining. You should all just count your lucky stars you are still alive. We don't take kindly to anyone refusing to serve in our army or trying to steal from our ships at sea. You all deserve what you are experiencing. We don't provide anything for you here. You can see the buckets against the wall. Someone will come to empty them once a day. A church brought over the blankets piled up there by the wall. You are all welcome to that and maybe they might bring some food. I stay out of that."

Joseph hoped someone would bring some food. The fellows here looked half starved. He walked over to the blankets and tried to find one that was not torn too much but he couldn't find a very clean one. It was late and everyone was asleep or in pain so he found a place where he could lay out his blanket and hoped he could get a little sleep. He was exhausted and it wasn't long until he was sleeping and dreaming of Joanna, wondering if she would ever know where he was taken.

Joseph woke up to the realization of where he was and the desperation he felt. Then he bowed his head in prayer and the Holy Spirit gave him peace that he would live and be able to escape from this terrible place. He looked around and noticed another man looking his way. He didn't look as pitiful as some of the others.

"Well, we have another day to go through, stranger. My name is Robert. Everyone calls me Bert around here. One thing I can tell you though….I saw your head bowed in prayer. That will get you nowhere around here. This is the next thing to hell if you haven't found that out already." Bert looked like he had been a very handsome man at one time. His red hair and sturdy build made Joseph think he had been in some strenuous work.

"My name is Joseph, Sir and I know that the only help I will receive is from the Lord. I can see we will not get any help from our jailors. There should be some laws and regulations of how to treat prisoners."

Bert laughed but he did come to be a friend of Joseph. He seemed glad that someone had some hope of getting out of there. Everyone did notice that there was food the guard brought in given by the Congregationalist Church so Joseph surmised John had been able to at least notify someone from the church. Even so they did not have enough food to go around and everyone was still losing weight. Days just went into each other until no one knew even what time of the year it was. They decided it was getting warmer in there and when the guard came in they could feel a warm breeze. July 4th came and the guard announced everyone was celebrating the Declaration of Independence. They all wished they had some of that Independence. Bert kept asking Joseph when his prayers would be answered.

It was August when Bert noticed through a slit in the window that there were some sloops close to shore. He motioned Joseph over wondering if they could possibly plan an escape. They decided to jump the guard when he came in next and head to the ocean and the sloops to escape. They gathered the prisoner sailors together just as the guard came in and he broke up their gathering and murmured as he left that it looked like those men were up to no good. Joseph and Bert decided they would take advantage of the next time the guard came because it would probably be no time until he would get some reinforcements. That would probably be early this evening when the shifts changed and the guard came in to check on the men before his relief arrived.

"Let's post two men, one on each side of the door and attack him with two of these buckets. I think, Bert, we should be the ones who accomplish this because none of these men seem strong enough to me to be able to carry this through." Bert agreed and they prepared to make this stand. They knew the guard was already suspicious so they wanted to do this before he persuaded his superiors to send him more help.

It was just getting dark when the guard came to finish his check before going home. He thought it seemed very quiet when he started to open the door but thought maybe they were all sleeping by now.

Joseph and Bert were ready with their buckets and the men were all ready to escape. It was so dark the guard couldn't see any danger as he pushed the door open all the way. He fell to the floor and Joseph with the help of Bert pushed him aside as the men all filed out of the room and headed for the ocean. A couple of the men needed help to get down there. Bert was hoping this was some of his comrades on the sloop at the ocean shore.

One of the sailors came ashore to meet their group. Bert was thankful it was one of his friends that he had worked with for years. When Jack realized that it was his friend he ran down the beach to meet him. "Bert, Bert…We gave up of ever seeing you again. In fact, I didn't even know you at first. Hurry so we can get away from here as fast as possible. I'm glad it is going on for darkness or we would never make it. Here, let me help some of these poor fellows," he said as he rescued a man down on the sand and half carried him to the sloop as Bert and Joseph helped some of the other men.

They were able to get everyone on board but Joseph could see the other sailors were not too pleased with their passengers. He knew they all looked a sight and smelled worse but he didn't know what to do about it. He thought they would probably be exited off as soon as possible. He just hoped their next destination would be Nova Scotia. Joseph turned to Jack, "We will all stay on this side of the ship. We know the sight we must be but we didn't get any food unless a church group brought it and we had no change of clothing. We attempted to wash them a couple of times last summer but that didn't turn out very well either."

"What did they lock you up for?" Jack asked. "I know you didn't get picked up for piracy. I found out you were all locked up but never knew what had happened," he said as he patted Joseph on the back. Bert found a little break to introduce Joseph to Jack.

"I was going to college, Jack. Then I was caught up in the draft. I didn't even know there was drafting in Connecticut in the first place and then I told them I wasn't a citizen in Connecticut and was there just to finish my education but they wouldn't listen to me. I've been in there for over a year. We couldn't take anything with us so what you see is all we have."

"I smell food cooking," Jack said as he walked over to a closet and brought out some blankets. "You will have to share these blankets. It is all I have. We should be coming into Nova Scotia in a day's time. We are heading for China next so anyone can come along with us there. We could use some more help." The cook brought in the soup he made and everyone was excited to have something to eat. Bert decided he would stay with his friends. He needed the work and he knew with this good food he would regain his health and be able to get back to working on the sea.

Joseph felt so weak at times he didn't know how he would make the long walk home when he arrived in Nova Scotia. He hoped Joanna had not given up all hope of ever seeing him again. He could just imagine how concerned his whole family was and also his Aunt and Uncle with their family. He could finally see the shores of Nova Scotia, his home and the place he had never wanted to leave. How beautiful it looked. September was always beautiful here. Bert stood beside him as they docked at the shore. "Good luck, friend. Maybe this is your prayers answered. It certainly seemed hopeless to me that we would every see the light of day."

"You can still change your mind and come home with me, Bert. Just remember God answers prayers and He will lead you and guide you in the right way. See if you can get a Bible and you can read his very words. I will be praying for you," he said as he shielded his eyes from the sun and looked to the shoreline of Nova Scotia.

Jack was seeing to the sloop and getting the shipment ready to deliver to the warehouse near the shore. As they embarked Joseph stepped off on shore and waved at everyone. He was on his way home.

Joseph stayed near the woods as he started walking home. He knew it would take most of the day to make the walk home. He stumbled and hit one of the tree roots as he walked. He wiped the blood off his leg with a few leaves and continued on. He couldn't wait to get home. He wanted to stay out of sight of anyone along the road. He was so ashamed of the way he looked and smelled. He knew God would be with him and give him strength to endure the walk. He stumbled again and lay in the leaves to rest awhile. It was getting dark by the time he arrived home. He could see his father walking in from the orchards. He didn't have the strength to call out but waved his hand to see his father look and quickly turn away to go up the stairs to go into the house. Joseph knew his father did not recognize him.

Susannah was dishing the food out for the family to sit down to eat. "Maybe you could dish another helping out and I can take it to the tramp I see coming up to the house, dear. He looks a sight and must be hungry."

Susannah quickly took down one of her old dishes and filled it with a helping of their meal. "I imagine it has something to do with this war in the colonies, David. I hear a lot of them are running off to avoid joining in the fight," she said as she handed the plate to David. "Now, children you all stay inside. Your father will take care of this. You never know if he is dangerous."

Mammy looked outside. She had come in to bring Daniel in to eat his dinner. "Don't you folks know who that is?" she said as she opened the door. Luci ran out all the way down the lane, wagging her tail all the way. Mammy ran after Luci, crying all the way, exclaiming, "Thank you, Lord Jesus, Thank you, Thank you." John ran out too. He was afraid Luci would try to protect Mammy and bite the man. She had been known to protect them from a couple men that were there to steal some of their apples late at night. She had them cornered until they were able to take care of them. Joseph knelt down and patted his friend. Mammy soon arrived and Joseph slowly stood and hugged her. "Oh, Joseph, whatever happened to you? I've been praying for you ever since you left here. So glad to see you again….so glad," and she proceeded to help him up to the house.

Susannah and David came out of the house and down the steps to meet them. They still did not recognize their son. They were perplexed about the whole situation.

Joseph was so worn out he could not talk. "Don't you see, don't you see, folks? It is your son come back home! It's your son. Praise the Lord." Mammy supported Joseph and young David ran to him. John continued to walk down in order to help his father bring Joseph in. Anne and Sarah brought in a tub and started warming up the water for him. They put it in the bedroom downstairs and ran out to greet their brother. Susannah ran upstairs to get clean clothing for their son. There was a lot of talking and rejoicing as they gathered around Joseph. Joseph looked up at David and whispered only one thing. "Papa, I carried out your wishes."

Chapter 6

Home Again

DAVID HELPED JOSEPH INTO the bedroom to take a bath. Joseph was so weak that he needed his father's help to remove the clothing he had on. He helped Joseph into the tub and prepared to bathe him but Joseph indicated he could do it himself so David left him, almost stumbling over Luci who was waiting at the door. "Luci will not leave, David," Susannah said as she handed David the clean clothing. David turned and put the clothing on the chair near the door. He saw Joseph dipping his whole head into the water as he closed the door once again. He petted Luci and went to sit down to wait for Joseph. He wanted to stay near in case his son needed him.

"I think we will wait until Joseph can eat with us," Susannah said. "I have everything set by the fire keeping warm." Susannah sat beside David as they waited for Joseph to wash off the extreme filth he was forced to live with for so long.

Mammy stood by but decided she should leave the family with David and see him later. She knew she would be taking a big part in his recovery. She wondered how long it would take him to recover. She just hoped the experience did not hurt his spirit but that when his health returned, he would be back to his own self. She knew his faith must have brought him through this experience. "Miss Susannah, I will go back to my cabin and see David in the morning. I have some sewing I can attend to also. I am just so glad God has answered all our prayers. It is so good to see him home again."

Henry was sitting by himself in the living room waiting for his brother to join them. He had always looked out for his younger brother. He always liked working with his father in the orchard and on the farm. He knew his red hair made people think he must have a bad temper but he was quite the opposite - gentle and quiet. He worked well with David and was involved in the young people's group at church. He was heartbroken for the way his brother looked coming home. He would not have recognized him but he was glad Mammy and Luci did.

Susannah knew Elizabeth along with Augustus and baby Lillie would come by as soon as they could. Elizabeth and Joseph had always enjoyed playing together as they grew up. Joseph would be so pleased with Lillie. He had missed out on so much being so far away from home and then jailed besides. The only news they had in all the over a year's confinement was what Mr. Bob could find out - and that hadn't been much.

Anne was silently crying. She had thought she would never see her brother again in this life. It had just seemed so hopeless. Her fiancée would assure her of the prayers going up on his behalf from the entire church congregation. She wished Calvin was here right now. He was the person she could depend on for comfort and hope through all this tragedy Joseph was in.

Sarah was sitting patiently waiting for Joseph to join them. Her head was bowed as she was thanking God for his return to them. She determined she would embroidery something to commemorate this day of rejoicing on Joseph's return. Joseph had always commented on Sarah's auburn hair and brown eyes. He always noticed her new projects. Sarah enjoyed needlework and everyone said God had given her the talent for the work she did with it.

Hannah and Susannah (Susannah was glad she had inherited her mother's name) were writing welcome posters for Joseph. They wanted him to know how much they missed him. They were making a background of Martha Washington's quilt, with a "Welcome Home" written with their best penmanship and with a pen dipped into their best ink. There were two years difference in their ages but they almost looked like twins with their black hair and blue eyes.

Young David, William and James were waiting patiently for Joseph to join them again. How they missed their big brother this past year and half, not knowing whether he was dead or alive. Daniel was walking now and running from one to another. He was wondering when they were eating their dinner.

"Do you need any help, son?" David asked as he sat by the door of the bedroom. He didn't hear any more water dripping. Knowing how weak Joseph was, he was worried about him. He didn't hear anything so he opened the door to see Joseph struggling to wipe himself with a towel. David went in to help and quickly closed the door. Joseph could barely speak. He whispered, "Help." David dried him off and sat him down in a chair while putting his clothes on. He wondered if he should just put him to bed or help him eat first. He decided to help him eat and then put him to bed. All the clothes were too large, especially the knee breeches but David did the best he could and led him to join the others in the dining room. Everyone was sitting around the table and they were excited that Joseph was once more sitting with his family. Joseph smiled at them and waved his hand at them all.

The girls helped Susannah put everything on the table. Tears were running down Susannah's face as she put the food on the table. She hoped Joseph could eat something and soon gain his strength back. She could hardly recognize her son even though he was clean now. The food was passed around but the atmosphere was sad and no one was talking. There was no noise except for the clattering of the pewter dishes. Joseph picked up a fork but was too weak to put any food on it or put it into his mouth. Susannah moved her chair over to his place and took the fork from his hand. He was able to eat a couple of bits but began to slump into his chair. His mother helped him with the glass of milk and then David and John helped him to the bedroom.

They had decided Joseph just needed more rest before he could eat with them or carry on a conversation. David gently covered his son with a quilt and quietly shut the bedroom door. The family finished their dinner and left the room. It wasn't long until Mammy appeared at the door. She looked as worried as the rest of the family. "Where is Joseph now, Miss Susannah? I had to check on him before I went to bed. I have never seen anyone in that condition. He has been mistreated…terrible, terrible, terrible. No, no, I will not come in unless you need some help with him," she said as Susannah motioned her to come in.

Susannah stepped outside to talk to her. She understood Mammy's grief for Joseph's condition. Mammy had always been her right hand help raising all her children. She knew Mammy had a special love for Joseph. He would spend a lot of time with her when he was growing up. He liked to hear all her stories of bygone days.

"Mammy, I will need your help with him tomorrow. I think for tonight we will just let him sleep. Maybe he will be much better tomorrow when he wakes up. He looks like he is starved not only for food but for rest also. I do not know all he has gone through. I would never have thought something like this could occur in our colonies. I know we are not a part of the conflict over there in the thirteen colonies but we have always felt like a part of their situation anyway. Please come back early tomorrow. I don't know what I would have done without you. I know you gave up a lot to be with us. I can't thank you enough," she said as she gave Mammy a hug.

Mammy was up early the next morning and had a chicken killed and cleaned for the soup she would make for Joseph. She knew chicken soup would help him regain his strength. She put it to cook on her small stove in her cabin and went to check on him.

It was 7 o'clock when she came to the house and everyone was up. Susannah was taking care of Daniel and the girls were fixing the breakfast. The boys were helping with the chores. Joseph was awake but still in bed. Mammy stood at the bottom of the stairs and called up to Susannah. "Is it alright, Miss Susannah if I look in on Joseph? I have some chicken soup cooking for him in my cabin. I thought it would give him strength."

"Mammy, thank you. Luci has been in there with Joseph all night and David has checked on him through the night. Could you ask one of the boys to let Luci out in the yard? You could sit with him today and I know you are trying to get some clothing ready for him so maybe you could do that. I appreciate your help. I have been praying for him that God would give him strength. I feel God has answered our prayers for him already."

"I will take care of it for you, Miss Susannah. I will just leave him long enough to get some of his brother's clothing and make them to fit. It was a miracle to see him come up that lane." Mammy left the stairway to check on Joseph. She found him still asleep. She couldn't believe how frail he looked. She said a prayer for him as she sat in the rocker by his bed. Seeing that he was completely covered she left the room to get William to take care of Luci and went to the cabin to get her sewing materials and a couple of knickers to take in for Joseph. She knew God would heal him and he would need the knickers soon. Luci seemed more relaxed and left the room to have William take him out.

By the time Mammy returned to the house Susannah was downstairs and preparing a dish of oatmeal for Joseph. She also had the bacon on to cook and the eggs in the basket the girls had just brought back from the hen house. Mammy brought the dish of oatmeal to Joseph and found him sitting on the side of his bed. He had been up already on his own and was holding on to the bed. He had used the facilities left him to take care of his morning needs. He was hungry and it was a comfort to know Mammy was taking care of him. He always trusted her to look out for him.

"So glad you sit up now, Joseph. Do you think you can eat your breakfast sitting on the side of your bed? I just been sitting here praying for you and starting to sew these things for you. We know you will need your rest today but we are hoping to see you improve every day." Mammy sat her chair in front of him and helped him with his oatmeal. He welcomed Luci back into the room. Luci seemed to think she was there to protect him from harm. Joseph wondered if he would have been better off if she had been there with him when they led him to jail. She never had bitten anyone ...just chased anyone off that she thought was up to no good. Usually it took one of the family to call her off before she would let them go. Her growl and appearance was enough to protect the family and the apple business. Joseph continued to eat the oatmeal although very slowly. He still didn't have the strength to walk out and join the family. Mammy helped him to lay down again and he immediately fell asleep. It had taken all his strength just to eat his breakfast. Mammy took the dish out to the kitchen and finding everyone about their duties for the day, came back to sit with Joseph.

It was about noon and Joseph was still sleeping with Mammy sitting in the rocker by his side. She had laid aside the last knickers she repaired and was darning some stockings she had found that would fit Joseph. She heard Miss Susannah in the kitchen. She knew everyone was out in the orchards today so she decided she could leave Joseph to help Miss Susannah put the dinner on the table. She could certainly fry some of the chicken and take some breaks to sit down in between. She left the room quietly.

Susannah heard the door and turned to see Mammy coming out. "How is he, Mammy? I have been praying all morning that he would recover. I wonder what all he has gone through to look this way. Did he say anything about his travel here or why he is in the state we found him?"

"He hasn't really said anything. He just been sleeping except for the time he ate his oatmeal and that was a struggle for him. He couldn't even hold the spoon. I helped him eat it," Mammy said as she took over frying the chicken. She could see Miss Susannah had already put the potatoes on to cook.

"Thank you for your help, Mammy. I don't know what I would do without you. The girls are out helping in the orchard," she said as she gave Mammy a hug. "I guess I'm depending on them too much anymore. I hope Mr. Bob will be able to get through today so that we can ship these apples. It seems like I haven't seen him in ages. It is dangerous with all those English war ships out there."

"Well, the only thing we can do is have meals ready for the workers and hope that Mr. Bob can get through soon. I always enjoy seeing him. He sure enjoys our apple pies," she said laughingly.

It wasn't long until everyone was in the house and ready to eat their dinner. Mammy said she would return to her cabin for a little rest and took a plate of food out with her to eat. She knew Joseph would be cared for with all the family inside for their dinner. Joseph woke up to the clatter of the pewter dishes as the family ate their dinner. They were speaking softly but Joseph heard them anyway. He walked to the door and saw them all sitting around the table eating.... something he thought he would never see again. Everyone stopped talking as they noticed Joseph at the door. David quickly walked to the door to help him.

"Here son, do you feel like sitting with us at the table?" he asked and with Joseph's whispered yes, he escorted him to sit down with them. "I have so much to tell you," he whispered "but I cannot do it yet." Susannah served him some mashed potatoes and stood by to help him eat. Joseph did better than he did eating the oatmeal but appreciated his mother's help as she dipped the spoon in and put it to his mouth. Joseph didn't stay long and David escorted him back to his bed. Of course Luci was right there with him and followed him back to the bedroom. David marveled at the faithfulness of this dog. When he came back everyone was talking. They were so concerned about their brother. Daniel was a couple years old now and didn't understand why Joseph looked like this.

"There are so many questions I would like to ask him, Mother," Hannah said. "He must have gone through so much to look in the condition he is in now. I wonder if Mr. Bob gets through with his sloop if he will know anything about Joseph's time in Connecticut."

David was wondering the same thing as the rest of his family. It grieved them all to see Joseph in this condition when he had gone from here in the best of health. In fact, they had missed him working with them in the apple business. His friends and all the church members had missed him when they had interesting sermons and the young people's activities. They all looked forward to hearing from Joseph about his experiences in Connecticut.

It was weeks before Joseph had the strength to communicate with his family and come to the table on his own. By that time the Second Continental Congress had signed the articles of confederation, November 15, 1777. The apples were ready to ship but Mr. Bob had not arrived to pick them up. They didn't know what was keeping him. Even the pirates were cooperating with the colonies and avoiding all contact with the British Navy. They were able to take on the cargo the colonies sent to different countries. Of course they insisted on excessive payment for their services.

"I am sorry for the worry I have caused all of you and I will try to tell you of my experiences in the last year," he said as he looked around the table at all his family. 'Each colony was assigned a number of men to be drafted. It was to make up for the lack of volunteers for the army. Some of the colonies had enough volunteers so they didn't have any to make up. Connecticut needed more men so they were drafting me. I told them my home was in Nova Scotia but they said since I was physically in Connecticut, that made me eligible for the draft. When I refused to serve they came to the house and took me away in handcuffs. I was a prisoner along with the other prisoners they had in tow. They walked us for many miles and when we came to the prison I was shocked at the state of that prison.

The smell knocked you over when you entered the place." Joseph seemed out of breath so Susannah brought him a glass of water and indicated to him to pause awhile as he went on with his recounting of these terrible events.

"We had to depend on other people to bring us food. They did not provide us with any. One of my friends who was going into the army notified the church that I was there and they brought in food but we had to share it with the other prisoners which didn't leave us much," he continued. "We got hungrier, dirtier, and more helpless as the days went by. Then one day one of the prisoners thought they recognized a sloop coming in. He was able to see it through a crack of the wood over the windows. We decided to jump the caretaker when he entered the door the next day. We were ready for him with our slop buckets. He was startled and went down when from each side we were able to dump the buckets on his head. We ran and were lucky enough to be able to get on that ship. "I think it was probably a success because of prayer, Joseph," Susannah said.

Joseph agreed with her and went on with his recounting of his experiences. He noticed Mammy had come in and was sitting with them. He was glad she had come in because he didn't want to go through this story again. "We were lucky that one of the prisoners knew the captain of the ship. He worked for him before his jail time and I think he was going to continue to work for him after they were successful in getting through all the English Navy ships out in the ocean. Some of the men with me died on the ship before we made it to Nova Scotia. I was so happy to step on Nova Scotia soil again. We were all so weak. I crawled most of the way here and tried to go through the woods when I could. I never will leave Nova Scotia again but I will have to make the trip back to Connecticut as soon as the war is over."

Joseph looked at his mother and father. "I am in love with Joanna and she promised me she would wait for me. We will get married right here at home. I know she will love it here." David and Joanna were startled but they knew Joanna came from a good family and they were anxious to meet her.

"I think we have tired you out, Joseph," Susannah said. "You must rest now. Thank you for telling us what you have been through."

"We will welcome Joanna here, Joseph," David said and walked over to give his son a hug. "When you are well enough, Joseph I think there will be a place for you in our business here. I still hope that you might continue to study law....maybe the way your Uncle Samuel did his studying. By the way, did you ever get a chance to talk to him personally?" he asked as he returned to his seat by the table.

"Uncle Samuel was in Philadelphia the whole time I was gone. He continues to work with the congress on different bills and other things. The second continental congress has approved a draft of the articles of confederation. Now everyone has to sign that before it can become a law. I saw his wife, Martha and their adopted daughter and son." Joseph was having trouble talking. He had used all his strength. He paused and then said, "I will go to lay down awhile. It is so good to see my family," he said. "It is so good to be home again."

CHAPTER 7
The Adoption of Our American Flag

IT WAS CHRISTMAS OF 1777 before Joseph was well enough to participate in family matters. He had missed the whole apple harvest and all the work and happiness it always brought the family. He didn't know the flag of 13 stars and 13 white and red stripes had been adopted by their congress. When he heard about this he knew his family was not as interested in this news as he was. He could picture the joy Joanna was feeling to know they had their own flag and that Betsy Ross had designed it.

Everyone in the colonies knew about Betsy Ross and her dedication to the cause of freedom. He would never forget the care his family had given him through his illness. Mammy had stayed by him continually through the worst part of his recovery. He was dressed warm on this Christmas Eve to help pick out their Christmas tree. Christmas Eve was always a very special occasion in their family. They all knew the reason for the season and were thankful for the Lord's guidance and love through the year. All the men and boys were going out into the snow and cold. The ladies and girls would stay inside to make cookies and get the decorations down. The candles were already laid out ready to put on the tree.

Joseph was the last one ready. William was knocking on his bedroom door. "Come on, Joseph! Everyone is ready. We need to get our tree." William didn't have to wait long. Joseph was ready to go. He was in a happy mood. He had given up ever joining his family in these fun things they did but with God's healing he was able to do the things he loved. Everything would be perfect if Joanna was here with him but he knew God had a plan for that also. He greeted William with a hug and teasingly ruffled up his red hair. He had to put his boots on and he would be taking his first trip out this year. David had the wagon all ready and was waiting for everyone. The horses were more than ready and stomping in place. David was so glad to see his son, Joseph ready once again to join them. Mammy was looking out her window and rejoicing that Joseph was able to go out with the other fellows. Every one of the children was dear to her heart.

God had really blessed David with this wonderful family. She knew that she had made the right decision so many years ago to stay with David and his family when she was offered her freedom. It wasn't long until she saw the wagon leave with David at the reins. It was wonderful to see Joseph sitting in the wagon as he did for years while growing up.

"I think I know just the tree you will choose, boys," David said as he encouraged the horses to get them to the evergreen forest. "We want to pick ours before we let the others in to choose their tree. I think the girls will like this one also. I almost picked this one last year but thought it needed to grow one more year." Joseph was not used to the weather yet and so he gathered the blanket around him to keep warm. There was a strong wind and he was wondering how the horses were keeping their balance.

In the meantime the girls were into the cookie baking. Little Susannah had her beautiful black hair tied back with a blue ribbon her Aunt had sent her last Christmas. She was a teenager now and was very excited about all the parties and dinners they would be attending for the Christmas holidays. Anne and Sarah were putting the first ones in the fireplace oven their father had made for them for baking. They were all looking after Daniel. He could walk well now and was getting into everything. They especially watched him as he approached the fireplace but he seemed to be eyeing the cookies most of all this morning. "Let me make the sugar cookies, Mother," Susannah said. They always cut these out to represent Christmas trees.

"That would be fine, Susannah. You can mix them up at the end of the table. Let Hannah do the fried cookies and I will make the Cinnamon nut bars. That is all we should make today. Sarah, I know you are working on some Christmas gifts but you can put that down for now and gather the eggs this morning. Thank you, everyone for all the help you give me. Now, I just hope they get a nice tree today."

Joseph was excited to see what tree had been chosen for this special Christmas. When they arrived at the forest everyone agreed their Papa had chosen the right one as they looked around at all the other trees. William and James even got out of the wagon to see if they liked another tree better but as they walked around they could not find any that looked half as good. They all stood around as David proceeded to cut the tree down. It always hurt Joseph to see any tree cut down but he knew that this tree had a wonderful purpose in their celebration of Christmas. He and Joanna would always teach their children the real meaning of Christmas. He hoped that someway, somehow he would be able to devote his life to working on the land and not be expected to go back to college to continue his education in law. He was very appreciative of all his Uncle Samuel had accomplished for his country through his education in Law. How he wished yet that George Washington had seen the value of accepting the help of the young men in Nova Scotia in the war with England. Everything was great but Joseph was missing Joanna. He didn't even know if Joanna had received the message that he had been rescued and home again in Nova Scotia. They didn't know when Mr. Bob would be able to get through the British parole to come to see them. Hopefully he would have news of Joanna and her family.

Susannah ran out to meet them when she saw the wagon return. She hoped the trip was not too hard on Joseph. Everyone ran out of the house to join Susannah as they waited to see the tree. They all were in one accord with their approval of the tree chosen. They would have to be very careful when the candles were lit and never leave the tree alone as long as it was lit up. The tree was put into a bucket of water and left in a cool place. Everyone was ready to sample a cookie in the making. They were so glad to have Joseph with them this Christmas, getting well but missing the love of his life. He knew this would be a long engagement because at this time it didn't seem like the colonies would win. Of course they had their own flag which was adopted by the congress in June of 1777 but a lot of the recruits had finished out their service times and left the army with only 1,000 men at the first of the year. By June they were up to 9,000 again with the new recruits so it was looking better according to Mr. Bob when he had come last summer with the news. Also Lafayette from France had volunteered and was training some of the troops for General Washington. It would be a good Christmas as it looked like the colonies had a chance at freedom as they waved their flag. Susannah was watching the cookies dwindle down and decided quickly to put them away before they all disappeared. They would be putting up the tree right after dinner with all candles and ornaments the children had made on it.

"You look exhausted, Joseph," Susannah said as she welcomed him back from their tree selection. "You need to go back to bed until dinner time." Joseph yielded to his mother's advice and went to lay down as he savored the experiences of their Christmas preparation. He wished Mr. Bob would come in to bring him a letter from Joanna. How he wished they could experience Christmas together. He knew that was impossible right now with the war going on and he would not let his desire to be with Joanna to spoil the family's Christmas. He would be thankful for the opportunity God had given him to be with the family. He was worn out but enjoyed his excursion in choosing the Christmas tree. He had so much to be thankful for. He thought he would have died if he had to spend one more day in that terrible jail. As he fell asleep, he thought of Joanna and wished Mr. Bob would bring her to him instead of just a letter from her. He woke up to sounds of the family gathering for their noon meal. He felt stronger now and joined them for the meal.

After David finished the blessing everyone was excited to get ready for their Christmas celebration. "Joseph, we even found the manger you made years ago. Even the baby Jesus that Sarah had made. Mother said we could put it outside and everyone would know what we are celebrating….that we know the reason for the Christmas we are celebrating….the birth of Jesus." William's eyes sparkled as he recounted their morning activities for Joseph. The girls had gathered up the candles and hand-made ornaments for the tree. David and Susannah wondered also why they had not seen Mr. Bob for a while.

They knew the trade ships were protected by an issue from congress that the American Navy was only authorized to attack the King's ships but to leave private ships alone. They thought Mr. Bob would want to go home to his family for Christmas.

The soup was delicious and tasted so good on this cold and snowy day. There was practice this afternoon for the children. Susannah had helped make some costumes for the shepherds and the wise men. William and James were excited to practice in their costumes today. It would be fun to walk over there in all this snow. Papa said they could walk today instead of riding over in the carriage. Mother planned to make the fruit cake today. She knew she should have made it before but with all the concern about Joseph she had put it off until the last minute. It wasn't long after their meal until the children were off to the church to practice for the Christmas program. It was left to Susie to look after the younger children as they walked to the church. They were tempted to run off into the snow and play instead of keeping their minds on the program they would be practicing for.

Susannah was finished mixing the fruit cake when she heard the sound of a horse coming up the lane. They had very few visitors this time of the year so she always was delighted when anyone would come to visit. She was surprised to see Mr. Bob riding up and ran to the door to welcome him. David heard him also and came running from the barn. "You can put your horse in the barn, Bob!" David called. "It is too cold out today for him outside." Susannah put on more coffee and put out her cookies while Mr. Bob took care of that. He was going to miss the children but at least Daniel was here with them. He was too young to be in the program.

David and Bob came into the house together. "How is Joseph? I hope he has recovered by now," Bob said. "You will see him when you come in, Bob. He is still weak but getting better every day. I know he is waiting for a letter from Joanna. I hope you have one there in the mail you are bringing in. It would have even been better if you could have brought her with you. You know how that is, friend. It looks like they will have a long, long engagement." Susannah had the door open for them when they arrived at the house.

Bob hurried in when he saw Joseph sitting there. "You are looking good, Joseph. I am so glad you can be up and around now. I hear you even went out to pick out your Christmas tree today. Great…I am so glad. Joanna sent a little gift to you also, Joseph," he said as he shook his hand and gave him a hug. This family had always meant so much to him. He would be overjoyed when this war was over and he would not have so much trouble with his trade ships. He also felt like he was kept away from his own family and all his friends.

"It is so good to see you, Mr. Bob. You don't know how glad I was to see the shores of Nova Scotia once again. It was my dream we would be part of the colonies and help them fight this war but that wasn't to be," Joseph said as he stood and gave Mr. Bob a grateful welcome.

"I was hoping for the same thing, Joseph. You have someone in the family who is fighting for their freedom. I saw your Uncle Samuel as the congress was leaving Philadelphia when the British took over. He still maintained that God was with them and they would obtain their freedom despite the illness and lack of provisions they faced now. I hear that George Washington even offered $10.00 for anyone who could form shoes out of hides. Mrs. Washington was living near the camp and instructing ladies in knitting socks for the men. Samuel and the other members of congress were in danger of losing their lives in even signing the Declaration of Independence and defying the King of England. Only by God's will they can be successful and win their freedom from England." Bob sat down at the table and distributed the mail from Connecticut.

"The Starr family are all well, David and of course Joanna wishes she could come here and join Joseph. She was devastated when he was put into jail and so relieved when he escaped. I don't think she realized how ill he was when he arrived here. Thank God he had the care and rest he needed to recover. I can see you are a lot better than when I saw you last, Joseph. I am sorry to tell you I would be afraid to take her with us and she would be going against her parent's wishes. It looks like you will have to go there for your wedding, young man. Her parents are very sure they want their daughter to be married in Connecticut. It will be fine with them if she comes back here after they are married. I would never want to carry any of them before this war is over. I know it seems like a long engagement but I know a couple who were engaged eight years before they were married and seem very happy now after more than twenty five years."

"I will wait as long as it takes and I know Joanna feels the same way, Mr. Bob. I am just happy you can bring us news of the family and bring me letters from my sweetheart. I will have an answer to this letter when you return." He couldn't wait until once again he could hold her in his arms. He wasn't looking forward to returning to Connecticut for their marriage but he knew he would do anything to see her once again and to be able to bring her back here to Nova Scotia.

"I need to get back to my family, folks," Mr. Bob said as he finished his coffee and stood to start his journey to his family. "They are expecting me for Christmas. Someday I will retire from this trade business and stay here in Nova Scotia. It is good to see everyone. Oh, I almost forgot, Joseph. Joanna sent this to you. She thought at least you could share a little bit in their freedom and fly this flag."

Bob gave him the new flag of red, white and blue. "I guess I will see the children when I come back after Christmas. I know all the decorations will look beautiful this evening and tomorrow. I have a few gifts for my family that I picked up in Connecticut. I am sure they will think Santa Claus has come to see them. Hopefully as we go into the year 1778 we will see peace once again. We need to depend on God to see us through this time. I hear France might send some help. We could certainly use it. They couldn't hope to compete against a strong military that England has unless God intervenes and brings them help."

As Joseph rolled out the flag, David escorted Bob out to the barn to get his horse and be on his way. Susannah was sorry the children were not home to visit with him. He had been such a joy to their family.

It wasn't long until Mr. Bob was on his way to his family and Joseph had the flag displayed on the wall near the fireplace. Everyone could see it and rejoice that the colonies were on their way to freedom.

The children were home later in the afternoon and were all pleased the way their play was going. Anne and Sarah were helping direct the play and were both excited about tomorrow afternoon when the play would be put on with the audience of the neighbors and church attendants round about. "Sarah's costumes fit all the children, Mother. You should see how beautiful it all looks. The Shepherds' costumes look so authentic. They have real sheep in the play also and they lead them out of the side door. They just used the small lambs."

Anne's blue eyes sparkled as she told of the way the play was going. Susannah was so excited she was jumping up and down. She was still holding on to her doll who would be playing the part of baby Jesus. She was glad to be asked to be Mary and holding baby Jesus.

"I am glad everything went so well with the practice. Let's put up our tree next. Susannah and David, do you think you are big enough to go out to get the tree? Papa will help you. We already have the stand waiting for it in the living room. Hannah, you can arrange the candles on it. The rest of you can string the popcorn and put on the decorations you all have made for it." The children hurried to follow their Mother's directions. David came in with the tree and his helpers and found it set perfectly in the stand without touching the ceiling. It wasn't long until the children had it all decorated and ready for their celebration. They would smell their mother's cooking by the fireplace.

Daniel was up from his nap and running around trying to get to the ornaments and popcorn that they had strung around the tree. It took James and William to look after him and keep the tree safe. William's red hair shone out in the setting sunlight as it glistened on the fallen snow. Susannah and David stood with their arms around each other, admiring the tree and the work their children had accomplished. They were so thankful for their family. "God is good, Susannah," David said, "His mercy endureth forever."

CHAPTER 8

The Almighty Ruler of The Universe

"The Almighty Ruler of the Universe raises up a
powerful friend among the Princes of the earth."
[George Washington]

MR. BOB DIDN'T ARRIVE back to the Nova Scotia Starr household until the end of February of 1778. He had stopped at their home on the way to Connecticut right after Christmas just long enough to pick up their answers to the letters he had delivered. He could see then the sadness in Joseph's eyes. Mr. Bob hoped this war would soon be over and Joseph and Joanna could begin their lives together. Luci was right at Mr. Bob's feet. She always was there to welcome Bob and he paid a lot of attention to her.

Mr. Bob shook hands with David and walked into their home after tending to his horse. "The trading went well, David," he said as he sat down, "but the war isn't going good at all. Washington and his men have suffered greatly at Valley Forge. So many of the men have given up and gone back home. There are good things happening also. Baron Von Steuben has arrived there and is training the soldiers. He said that no European army could have held together in such circumstances. I have faith that God will lead them through this and that they will obtain their freedom."

David always kept an open mind but still held with his church that they would remain neutral. He was glad Joseph had been able to escape from Connecticut even though he had suffered so through the jail experience and the trip here to Nova Scotia. He knew he needed to change his expectations for his son and he would be talking to him about that soon. "I know you have seen a lot more of their struggle than we have here, Bob. Joanna and Joseph are waiting for the news of victory in the colonies for more reasons than most. I keep praying for God's will to be done."

Susannah and Hannah came into the room where David and Bob were discussing the war situation. "I thought I heard your voice, Bob. Can we get you some coffee or did you have dinner yet? We had ours a couple hours ago but I could warm something up for you. We are always so glad to see you. I am surprised Joseph isn't here to see about what you know of Joanna," she said as she put the clothes she carried on the end of the table. "Hannah, you can fold these clothes and put them away, please." Hannah immediately started folding the clothes. They smelled so fresh from the fresh air where they were hanging since this morning.

"Your family is growing up so quickly, David. I remember when Hannah was just toddling around here. She is turning into a beautiful and sweet young lady." Hannah was blushing with the compliments. "And we are growing older, David. I see the gray streaks in your hair and the same in mine." They all laughed about that and as they were laughing Joseph came out of his room. "It is so good to see you, Joseph." Bob walked over and shook Joseph's hand. "I never thought to see you looking so well. It shows God's answer to our prayers. From hardly recognizing you to seeing you as a young, handsome man is more than we could have asked. I wish you could join Joanna but I am afraid you will have to wait until this war is over. It is too dangerous to try to give you transportation over to Connecticut at this time. Sit down, Joseph. I can see you don't have all your strength back yet."

Susannah moved a chair out for Joseph so he could hear all the news Mr. Bob had for them. "I am feeling stronger every day," he said as he sat with them. "Between everyone's prayers and all the kind care my family gives me, including Mammy, I think I will make it. I plan to work with the orchards and fields this spring. I have missed it so much these past couple years. How are Joanna and all the family, Mr. Bob?"

Bob smiled as he told him but for missing the most important person in her life Joanna was quietly waiting for the war to be over and she could begin their life together. "There is also good news of this war. France has recognized the independence of the United States. This step means the French will join in the war against Great Britain. The thirteen colonies are no longer alone."

"I wish Nova Scotia could have been part of that, Mr. Bob but I know that was not in God's plan. It should have all been settled peacefully as our church has indicated," Joseph said as he stood from his chair. "I realize now that Britain has done a lot for us through the years as my brother, Samuel will tell you but they should realize that the colonies have become too large to be colonies and subject to a King overseas. I would have gladly served if Nova Scotia had joined in the conflict but as I said that wasn't to be."

"I think I will pass on anything to eat, Susannah. I need to get home and see the family. It will not be long until I will be picking up the apples and pears to take back to Connecticut with me where they will be shipped all over the colonies. I guess I better stop referring to them as colonies as they think of themselves as the U.S. of A. and they are proud to call it that. I think with the French Fleet out there in the ocean now we will have a better time getting through. I will leave these messages for you now and be on my way. I hope you will be able to participate in the work out there, Joseph. I have been noticing the orchards as I came here and they look like they are healthy trees and not suffered too much through the winter. I know you have the fields to tend also. God bless you all as you work together." Bob started toward the door with Luci on his heals ready to get his horse and leave. Everyone knew Luci needed to see Bob off but she would be right back as soon as Bob left.

David waved at Bob as he left and then turned to Joseph. "I need to show you some farm things, Joseph. Come with me to my desk. Let's let the young folks settle around the table to study. I know your Mom will think she is behind in teaching them this afternoon but it was good to see Bob again. I am glad he will be a little safer in his trade business with the French Navy out there also." Joseph followed David to his desk in another room he had set up for his farm concerns.

When they were seated David took out the paper work he wanted to show Joseph. "First of all, Joseph, I want to tell you I am very sorry about pressing you into preparing for a profession of law when as far as your mental capabilities you would have made a good and fair lawyer. I felt that God had given you the talents to carry out that career. I realize now that you should not choose a work for anyone even if it is your son. I can see now your heart is in the land and you would never be happy as a lawyer. Even the living arrangements in these towns and cities would suffocate you. I know one fellow that lives in the city now told me he felt like he was living on top of his neighbors and had no privacy at all. Uncle Samuel educated himself with the library of Rev. Ebenezer Devotion and was always grateful for the use of his books. He was able to follow his dreams while being apprenticed to a cooper and helping his father on the farm. I know you saw him when you were very small but through going to Connecticut you were able to get better acquainted with him. I hear he continues to represent Connecticut in Congress and we are very proud of him."

"I wish, Papa, I would have been able to follow your wishes but I never felt like that was God's plan for me. I did see Uncle Samuel and Aunt Martha. I guess you knew that his brother, Joseph died and they adopted their niece and nephew and I know that they have a very loving home with their aunt and uncle. I met them before the officials picked me up for refusal to join the army. I don't know if he could have helped me or not but I was never allowed to contact anyone. I couldn't even contact my church. I had to rely on another friend – the one I told you about before - who contacted his church and they did bring in food for us. Anyway, Papa, I have always felt very close to God as I worked with you on the farm and the orchards. I know that is what I was meant to do. I can always help at the church whatever seems best too."

David handed over some of the papers he was looking at as Joseph was talking to him. "I accept your willingness to work with me, Joseph. It will soon be time to prepare the fields for the crops. I have been working on these planning papers all winter to determine what we will plant this year and in what field. I would want you to look them over and when you are strong enough to be out in the fields with me to accomplish all of this I know you will be a real help to me. I'm having trouble doing all this paper work connected to farming and you will be a real asset to me in that area. These diagrams show the way we drain the water from the fields into the ditches. The spring can get very wet if we don't take care of the drainage system. Through generations we have developed a system whereby we can grow the crops that have the most yield and Bob can obtain for us the best price for our crops when he delivers them to the colonies - or I should say the United States of America. Harvesting time is real busy but we have good farmers in our neighbors and as you know we all join in and have our Harvest Dinners together."

Joseph was happy to have this talk with Papa. He finally felt accepted in the work he was so interested in doing. "I noticed when I was in Connecticut, Papa, that they are a little ahead of us in their seasons. They seemed very let down when their corn was not knee high by the fourth of July. I think we are happy with it if the corn is that high by August 1st. I hope Anne will be happy here so far from her family," he said as he looked to his Papa for advice.

"I know, Joseph, that you had dreams of us joining with the other colonies in this revolution but we had no cooperation in George Washington or our governors here. We didn't even send a representative to the first or the second continental congress in Philadelphia. I think Anne will feel right at home here because she knows a lot of the people coming from New England to settle here. When you look around at our beautiful countryside and you enjoy the presence of our Congregational Church and all the inspiration and comfort it has provided you would not understand living anywhere else in the world. We take with us the values of generations of our Scottish ancestry and have established this colony of New Scotland. I hope that history will carry on in future generations of Starrs and all our relatives here."

David opened another drawer of the desk and showed Joseph all the diagrams of the land and the designated crops and positions of the water system. He looked up and saw Luci waiting patiently at the doorway to have Joseph's attention. He gave her the signal to come in and immediately she came over to lie at the feet of Joseph.

Joseph leaned down to pet her. Susannah brought in the package Johanna had sent with Bob. Joseph looked up to see William and James along with Daniel right there to see what was in the package. He pulled out a flag....the flag of Connecticut ...and a note from Joanna. The flag was hand-stitched to represent their flag. It was beautiful with the blue background and the white shield with three grapevines, each bearing three bunches of purple grapes. The state's motto was embroidered on it stating "He who transplanted sustains us" displayed on a white ribbon. They all knew the grapes are symbolic of good luck, felicity and peace - evidence of God's kindness and the goodness of providence.

"Papa, we will need to have a flag of Nova Scotia up there alongside of the Connecticut ones before Joanna comes here. Maybe Sarah could make one for us."

David laughed as he stood up. "I will leave you now, Joseph so that you can read your letter from Joanna in privacy. Remember to ask me any questions you might have of all the paperwork I have shown to you. The Title for the properties are there also and our land grants."

David left the room to join Susannah and the children looking over the mail Bob had left. "There is a letter from Joanna to us also, David. She seems to be a very sweet girl. I am sure this war situation is very hard on her. Even with the French ships out there now I don't think Bob thinks it would be safe to bring Joseph to Connecticut and then also he would still be on the list of escaping from jail. It probably would have been easier for him to bring Joanna here but I know her parents will not consider that at all. They insist that they be married at her home and I don't think they will ever consider any other way."

"It is only natural, Susannah, to want your daughter to be married at home," David said as he took a place at the table. "I wouldn't want her to travel here by herself either. Joseph needs to be with her when she makes that trip. We can always have a reception here for them when they arrive back after the war is over. I don't know when that will be. You hear so many conflicting reports. I will be glad when it is over and we can get back to normal again."

Joseph continued through the spring keeping track of the paperwork and even going out to help in the fields and orchards for a short period of time. He especially noted the diagram of the south forty where the ditches and drainage were all indicated to enhance their success in farming this year. His work would be more in the leadership capacity than it ever was before with David taking up the slack of his last stages of recovery from his experiences in getting home from Connecticut. He could always feel Mammy's watchful eyes on him. She kept thanking God that he was getting so much better. Bob stopped in to get their reply to the letters but they hadn't seen him since March and it was already going into July. They hoped he hadn't encountered any trouble at sea.

On July 4th they remembered the gift of the flag and Sarah hung the Nova Scotia flag she had made on the other side of the fireplace. Their loyalties were divided between the two countries.

It was the morning of the 10th of July when David recognized Bob coming up the lane with his horse. The horse was stumbling and Bob was walking up the lane. David ran down to see if he could help him. "Let me get to the house, David and then I will tell you all about it. I didn't think I would ever see Nova Scotia or my family again. God brought us through, God brought us through," he muttered as David led him to the porch and Joseph took care of his horse.

Bob sat down in the rocker and leaned his head back. "It's an Atlantic Naval war out there, friend. Our sloop is just about torn apart. You will not know how we survived when you see it. We did lose one of our sailors. Admiral Lord Howe is behind the whole situation. The French are helping the patriots but they don't have the ammunition they need. Then there was a Wyoming massacre on the 3rd of July. The Tories came in with a fierce band of Iroquois Indians and took 227 rebel scalps. Now I hear Admiral Lord Howe is out in the Atlantic with his ships and seems to be making progress against the patriots there. The French fleet is out there helping but the wind is in the wrong direction to be of any use to them. I don't know how that will all turn out but they still fly their red, white and blue flags and say God is with them and they will have their freedom from King George."

Bob stood again wanting to see his family and get back to help the men repair the sloop. "I'll stop back on my way back to sea, friend but I need to get back to my family and let them know I survived the battle out there," and he shook hands with David. Joseph took hold of his hand and said, "I hope George Washington isn't getting discouraged with all this trouble. It seems like things are going well and then something like this happens."

"Don't lose hope, Joseph. I hear George Rogers Clark did have a victory at an English settlement so we never know. I think Washington has had a lot of disappointments but he is a praying man and he just keeps carrying on with the men and ammunitions he has available."

They looked up to see Sarah leading his horse to the hitching post. Sarah's brown eyes sparkled as she looked up at the horse. Thunder seemed to know all the family and willingly let Sarah lead him to Bob. Bob walked out and took the rein, giving Sarah a hug for her tenderness with the horse. He could tell she had put some kind of lotion on his hoof. Luci was right there to see Bob off again. As Bob mounted his horse and waved goodbye to everyone Luci followed down the land. The family knew she would be back as soon as she saw Bob on his way home. Mammy was out in the yard waving also. She knew Susannah would share the letters that Bob brought with her. She was glad they accepted her as part of the family.

David and Joseph went out to the orchards to get ready for the apple harvest and the children went with them to pick up apples that had dropped off before the pickers would be there. Susannah had the girls help her with the preparation of the dinner. The butter still had to be churned and the milk had to go through the separator while the others started the dinner preparation.

CHAPTER 9

1779 - Samuel Huntington Appointed President of the Continental Congress

THE STARR FAMILY IN Nova Scotia was waiting for a visit from Mr. Bob but they heard so many reports from the colonies that the seas were not safe. It was July of 1779 when they heard John Paul Jones had declared from the deck of the Bonhomme Richard that he had not begun to fight. They took the Serapis captive and somehow the Americans were winning the war.

Joseph continued to improve and knew that he would soon be as well as he was before he had ever went to Connecticut for his education. Mammy was so pleased with his recovery. She was happy also with the work Joseph did within his Congregationalist Church, especially with the young people. In all the work in the orchards and his interest in the Church, Joseph kept his eyes on the results of the war. It seemed at times that the Americans were giving up but George Washington seemed to have faith that they would win. Joseph knew his dreams would not be realized until the war was over and Joanna would be able to come to Nova Scotia. He wouldn't feel complete until they were married and established their own home. Here it was well into 1779 and no news from his sweetheart. He filled his days out in the orchards and fields. He had been busy in the spring opening the dykes after the winter time also. There was so much work to do that he didn't know why his father fought the idea of him spending his life on their land. It had worked well for his mother and father in raising their family. It should work for Joanna and him also. He couldn't wait for her to see the beauty of Nova Scotia.

The men were coming in from the fields and the children came running in from playing. They had a few months off from their schoolwork. Everyone was looking forward to the new school building which would be finished by fall. Susannah would be able to take a break from teaching. She and the girls had the meal all ready for the men after they washed up for their evening meal.

Young Susannah came in with the rolls she had made herself. "Papa," she said, "I hope you like the rolls." David admired his daughter's bright blue eyes. She always seemed to be sparkling. You could tell she enjoyed cooking with her mother. She was ready for high school subjects already.

"You know I always enjoy anything you cook, honey. In fact I don't know what I would do without any of you. This is the way everything gets done around here. I like your new apron, too. Did you make that yourself?" David loved all his children and was proud of their accomplishments. He liked the way Susannah encouraged them all to live up to their potentials. They were each one so different and interested in working in different areas although they all enjoyed working in the orchards.

"You know who made this apron, Papa, with all the embroidery on it. While I am slaving over this stove Sarah is sitting over there sewing for us. She knew I like tulips so she embroidered these tulips on the pocket. She has a talent that I don't have."

"You know she would teach you how to do it, Susan. But then we wouldn't have these delicious rolls." Papa was the first to sit down as Anne brought in the roast and potatoes. Everything looked delicious and the vegetables came right out of their garden. Little William was so proud of making the dessert under his mother's supervision. He had mixed up the chocolate cake and cleaned the bowl after putting it in the pan to bake in the oven David had constructed over the fireplace. William's freckles really showed up in this heat. He and Henry were the only ones with red hair.

Susannah finally sat down when everything was on the table. The girls had helped her so much setting the table and helping with the food. "David, would you ask the blessing so we can eat this food when it is still hot?"

David and the members of their family joined hands as he prayed. "Heavenly Father, we thank you for the many blessings you have provided for us. We know our efforts would not amount to anything but you cause the crops to grow. We only plant them and take care of them. We pray that you will continue to provide the good weather we need and the orchards will flourish so that we have good fruit crops also. We haven't seen Bob for months. We know he is in danger out there at sea and we pray for his protection. We also pray for our future daughter-in-law, Joanna and that you will make it possible soon for her to join Joseph here. We now thank you for this food and the strength it provides for us. In Jesus name, Amen."

The meal was noisy as usual with the movement of the pewter dishes and serving bowls. Daniel added his words such as they were from his wooden high chair. He would soon be outgrowing his high chair and would be learning along with the other children. He already could color and seemed to have a gift for art. Everyone was talking about the new school and who would be the schoolteacher. Susannah was looking forward to having help teaching. Anne and Sarah already helped her a lot with the schooling. Anne was looking forward to her marriage soon and Sarah was being courted by a childhood friend. No one knew how that was all going to turn out.

"I think we would have time tomorrow, Joseph to work on the house. Maybe we can get it framed. The foundation is all finished and Henry down the road said he would be able to give us a hand." David was finished with his meal and ready for his dessert. William was more than ready to serve it. "It is still light out also so maybe we have enough light to practice some ball."

David and his sons were up early the next morning except of course, James and Daniel. David would get them out there as soon as possible helping him in the fields, the stock, the orchards and then the building when that came about. His sons couldn't remember the day when they didn't help their father with the work and chores around their property. They had a full life between their studies, work and then the church where they helped as soon as they were ready.

"Who will live in this house, Papa?" William asked as he looked up at David with the trust and love that he always had for his father. David looked down at his son and couldn't help but notice that his freckles were getting more prominent as the weather continued to be very hot.

"It will be a home for Joseph and Joanna, William," David said as they walked to the barn to get the horses out and the wagon to carry their equipment and lumber to the building site. "We need to have it ready when the war is at least under control and Mr. Bob can transport Joseph back to Connecticut to marry Johanna. Then he will bring them both back here to live."

Joseph was following the group, more excited than any of them. God was answering his prayers. He knew that all the Lord had led him through so far in his life that this would only be another place he could say that God led him through. He still was in favor of the American cause and prayed for the patriots there every day. He knew it just wasn't God's will that Nova Scotia be a part of it. Maybe it was better this way….his brother, Samuel was serving in the British Navy so they would never be fighting against each other. He knew that would break his family's hearts. Joseph ran to catch up with his father and brother to load the wood, the bricks and building materials onto the wagon.

There was something for everyone to do and by the end of the day they had the house framed in. The building blocks were stacked up and ready to go the next time they had a day to work on the house. David knew Susannah wanted a wrap-around porch on the house so he had made provisions for that also.

Susannah and the girls were busy all day also. "Now that the men are gone to the new house let us get this quilt done for Joanna." Susannah got all the fabric out from her hiding place. She didn't want Joseph to see what they were working on either. "I think we have everything cut out now and the blue stars are put on the blocks. They are all on a white background and then….Oh, Sarah, there are a few that have not been sewed on yet. Would you take care of that? And Anne maybe you can cut the rest of the red stars out….. these go in between the blocks with the blue stars. The rest of us will lay out the blocks on the quilting table and maybe we can get it all sewed together and ready to quilt next time we get together to work on it. I know she will love it. It will always remind her of her homeland and we know they have paid dearly for their freedom there in Connecticut and all over the colonies. Just as we learned in our Bible studies though if God is with you victory can be achieved."

Sarah immediately started completing the rest of the blue stars and Anne was cutting while the others were laying out the pattern of blue on white and sewing on the red stars in between. They sent enough food for the workers' noon meal but would have to be ready for the dinner in the evening. Susannah hoped the men and boys would get a lot done on the house today. It wouldn't be long until David would need all his workers in the orchards and the fields.

David had also started on furniture for Joseph and Johanna. It would take a large quilt to cover the wide bed he was making for them. After hours of work they all stood around it with awe. It was exactly the way they pictured it would be. They could just imagine Martha Washington designing the quilt blocks. They knew Johanna would love it. They had it all assembled on top the basic backing with the batting inserted. It should work out well when they gathered around the floor frame again to do the quilting. The girls were anxious to get it done but Susannah told them they would need more hours to get any quilting accomplished. She said, "You will all see the outline of the stars on the backing when we get it finished. Have a few minutes to relax and then we will have to get the dinner on for the men coming in from the building site."

It wasn't long until they heard the noise of the wagons, the horses and all the fellows coming in. Susannah saw that the dinner was ready on time. The rolls were just out of the oven and the pies were cooling on the window sill. Everyone was washing up at the pump before they would come in. They left their shoes at the door to avoid tracking in all the dirt. "It's all ready for the brick work, Susannah," David reported as he came in. I know you were all working hard also." Susannah put her finger to her lips. She didn't want Joseph to know what they were doing. She wanted Joseph to be surprised along with Johanna. David quickly dropped the subject. "The neighbors can stay also, David. I have plenty made. I should have enough with all the help I get from the girls. Of course Daniel caused some disruption but he was good for his age. He still likes to investigate."

David laughed and sat down by the table. "I think everyone else went home, dear. They all said they were expected at home. It will just be our own family."

As usual you could hear the noise of the pewter and the conversation of everyone telling about the day's events as they ate. "I guess you didn't see anything of Mr. Bob, did you?" David asked. "I know we didn't see anything of him where we were. I don't know what we will do if he is not here at Harvest Time. That will start next month. I hope he can get through but I don't want him to take any chances either. I'm glad the Patriots are acknowledging our neutrality and not giving us any problems with it. So many of us came from Connecticut or Massachusetts I thought they would expect us to fight along with them regardless of Washington's inability to help us. I thought he would expect us to find our own equipment and men to fight along with them. I am glad they realized that we couldn't do that and accepted our stand." Everyone agreed that the Church's stand was best except Joseph still wished it had been different.

Sarah sat down to work on her sampler after dinner. The next day was Sunday so they were all laying out their clothes for the church service. Anne was only putting out one petticoat. It was so hot. Sarah planned to wear her new shoes. The cobbler had made them up for her last week. She measured them and they were exactly a match so it shouldn't matter what foot they went on. Sometimes she had one that was a little smaller and it fit better on her right foot. Susannah had the stew already made and keeping warm on the edge of the fireplace for the next day's meal after the church service.

Sunday proved to be a very enjoyable day with the fellowship of all their church members and the inspiring sermon. The dinner was delicious as usual. There was a lot of talk about the war situation and what it would mean to their trade with the colonies especially. Everyone was wondering about their vegetables and fruits, wondering if there would be a market for them.

It was October of 1779 toward evening before they saw Mr. Bob coming up the lane leading Victory. Joseph saw him first and ran out to meet him. He was most anxious to get the mail but his father was trying to keep the fruit good so it could be shipped when Bob next went out with his sloop.

Bob seemed to be limping as he approached Joseph. "We had all kinds of trouble," he yelled before he even came up to Joseph. Victory looked like he had seen better days too. "I will tell you all about it when we get to your home," he said as he struggled on and Joseph helped support him. Bob's breeches were torn. The rest of his clothes were all dirty, nothing like he usually came from the sea. Joseph knew his mother would have a meal warming up and a cup of coffee ready for him when they came into the house.

Susannah met them at the door and gave Bob a hug as he sat down on the nearest chair at the table. Everyone gathered around and Susannah placed a cup of coffee in front of him. Joseph took care of Victory.

Bob looked around at his dear friends. "Pirates boarded our ship but they were really looking for the British ships. They thought we were in favor of England so they started beating us up and were about to take our materials off the ship when they decided to take our word and protect us as Patriots. We thought we would lose our lives for a while. They knew that the Continental Congress had given them permission to attack and subdue all vessels belonging to subjects of the King of Great Britain but that they were to protect friends to the American cause. They finally decided to help us instead of taking advantage of us." Bob stopped and took a drink of his coffee. He opened his pack of mail and put it in front of Susannah to distribute it among the family. Of course, most of it was addressed to Joseph. "There is good news too, David. When John Jay was appointed as U.S. minister to Spain it left the office of President of Congress open and they appointed your nephew, Samuel Huntington to replace him. I expect he will eventually be the first President of the United States. I know the people in Connecticut are really behind him. He really gets things done although he is a very shy and humble person. I wonder if that doesn't come from his Christian testimony and his connections with the Congregationalist Church."

David picked up his coffee while Susannah served Bob his meal which she had warmed up for him. "I know he was always a staunch member of the church. He married Martha Devotion, the Pastor's daughter."

Joseph came out of his room where he was reading his mail. He wondered how long he would have to wait to see her. Their house was almost ready. He knew it would be livable by winter. "Does it seem to be any better for me to go to Connecticut, Mr. Bob? It seems forever to wait to see Joanna again."

"I would like to think the recruiters would have already forgotten all about you, Joseph, but I don't know. I have thought of disguising you in some way but then we are taking a chance." Bob took another bite of the delicious food Susannah had put in front of him. "You know they are looking for traitors and Tories but the war is now going in the colonies favor so they might have let up on that. I don't understand how George Washington has kept the military going at all but I know God has the answers. I will go home for a week and think this all over so have your produce all ready, David."

David went out to see if Victory was ready to travel. Young David was almost a teenager now and had been feeding the horse and tending to his paw. He had a real love of animals and you could see him working out in the barn quite often. When you entered the barn he would look up at you with his beautiful brown eyes and friendly smile. Bob could see Victory was ready to go and so he bid everyone goodbye.

"The men are fixing the sloop as we speak, David. They should have everything ready when I come back through here. I will try to think of some way so Joseph could come back with me. Tell him to be ready just in case. It is some better out at sea and we do have the pirates' protection of what good that is I have yet to find out. It did get us out of this last problem." Young David gave Victory a parting pat and with a wave they were on their way.

CHAPTER 10

The Battle of King's Mountain Changes the Course of The Revolution in The South

THE STARR FAMILY ALL waved goodbye to Mr. Bob in "79" as he returned to Connecticut but were wondering again when they would see him as it turned to October in 1780 before they saw any signs of him. David was able to sell a lot of his produce right there in Nova Scotia but now he had all his apples picked and no market except for the few he could sell round about him. They all kept praying that the war would be over soon. Joseph didn't even feel like eating thinking about Joanna and wondering if she was still safe in this war. Mammy continued to watch over him and was concerned. He was doing so well through the harvest and she thought he had recovered completely but now seemed to be going down.

The sun was going down and they were all sitting around the table enjoying their meal as usual this day in the middle of October when Joseph noticed a horse and rider coming up the lane. "I see someone coming down the lane. Could that be Mr. Bob and Victory? It sure looks like him," he said as he pushed back his chair and went to the door. "It is him! Put another plate on the table, Mother. I imagine he is really hungry."

Joseph grabbed his coat and went running out. Everyone was excited that they would see their friend again. They kept praying that he wouldn't be hurt and God would protect his sloop.

Mr. Bob looked almost jubilant as he approached Joseph. "I'll tell you all about it, Joseph when I get in your home. I have some good news." Joseph took the reins and greeted Victory as he took him up to the barn to feed and rub him down. Victory seemed happier today also. "They are sitting a place for you at the table, Mr. Bob. Sit right down and I will be in soon." He took care of Victory and gave him a parting pat as he ate.

Bob was sitting with the family eating his meal when Joseph came in. "I waited until I could tell everyone the good news at once, Joseph. "The war is not over yet but it is coming to an end. They were worried if they would win the war there would be only ten colonies in the new United States but there was a battle on King's Mountain in South Carolina that has turned the war around. It was the American Tories that decided to go against the patriots. I am sure George Washington was really pleased with the results. The patriots took over 800 prisoners and British Major General Patrick Ferguson was killed along with others fighting for England. I think it would be safe now to get you, Joseph, over to Connecticut. I thought you would be ready when I come through again. You and Joanna could plan your wedding. You would be dressed as one of our sailors. When we come back Joanna would dress the same way. Even the pirates would help us against the English ships. I know the war will be over soon and it is past time they would be looking for recruits for their army. I'm willing to take the chance if you are. I think you have both waited long enough."

You could tell Susannah was concerned feeling they were taking a chance in taking Joseph with them but then she didn't know how long Joseph would hold up away from Joanna either. She didn't want him to get sick again. He had done so well throughout the harvest. She didn't know what David would have done without him. Samuel still served in the English navy. She was so glad none of their relatives who were patriots in Connecticut had ever come against him. Henry had helped his father so much but he was only one person. John was so good to oversee the trade. Joseph had been a great help to his father. It was comforting to Susannah to know he would be right there along with Joanna to see their endeavors would continue through generations. Young David was starting to be a big help although he would get distracted when the young people from church had something special to enjoy and he was in the field or the orchards.

Joseph looked over to his mother, "What do you think, Mother? Would we have the clothing to dress me like a sailor?" Susannah could see he had already decided to go. She would not keep him back. "You would make a good sailor, Joseph. We will dress you like one but you better get instructions from Mr. Bob of your duties. You want to act the part." Joseph appreciated his mother giving him her blessing on the trip.

"We are on our way to finishing the house also, Joseph," David said. "It is mostly the inside we have to work on now and we can do that as it is cold outdoors and it will soon be snowing." David didn't know how he would have lived this many years without Susannah. He prayed that God would bless their marriage as he had blessed theirs.

"I don't like to eat and run but I am anxious to see my family again," Bob said as he put on his coat ready to leave. "I'll leave this mail with you and when I return we will take your products with us. I will be glad when we can go into the waters without this war in the background. I'm glad the Americans will get their free country but I am glad we stayed neutral in this conflict. You know, we have friends on both sides and when I heard how many Tories had died in that last conflict I couldn't help but be sorry for all the families touched by this. A lot of them were planning on moving here but stayed to see how the war would go. Naturally they were living there for quite some time so they were not anxious to make such a move either."

"Before you go, Bob, let's all join hands and pray," David said as they joined hands around the table. Even little Daniel joined hands with them.

"Heavenly Father, You have protected Bob so often as he traveled the seas. We thank you for his help and his friendship. We depend on you for the right weather, the right seeds, the bees that pollinate our fruit trees, the strength to bring our crops to fruition we thank you. We thank you for our family and now we put Joseph in your hands that you will see him through this under the supervision of Bob. Through Jesus you have saved us from our sins. You have loved us throughout our lifetime and we see your hand every day of our lives. You lead us as a church and we know even the angels in heaven rejoice over one sinner that comes to repentance. We have seen that happen countless times. Thank you that the Holy Spirit has spoken to their hearts. Now, we depend on you to protect Bob as he joins his family. We know this has been a long time for them. Thank you, dear Lord for leading us and guiding us through our life. In Jesus name, Amen."

Bob bid them all goodbye and mounted Victory to go on his way home. It was dark by the time he started out. Daniel was soon in bed while the girls cleared the table and washed the dishes as they discussed what the sailors wore on the trade ships. "I guess Joseph would know. He traveled all that way when he came home from Connecticut," Sarah said. "I think I can design one and we could cut up one of his breeches. I think if we cut his cassock off a ways we could get the right outfit for him."

Sarah's brown eyes sparkled as she planned how she would sew the clothing he would wear. Everyone trusted Sarah to design just the right outfit for him as they had seen all the beautiful pieces she had designed for their home. So many of them were framed and hung on the walls. "Joanna wrote that our grandmother was making her wedding dress. I hope she will bring that along with her. You know we will not see their wedding. I wonder if Uncle Samuel and Aunt Martha will be there to see the wedding." They all wished they could attend the wedding but Joanna's parents insisted the wedding would be there so that they would feel better having her traveling with Joseph to Nova Scotia.

Susannah came into the kitchen. "I heard you talking about the wedding. I don't think Uncle Samuel will be able to go to the wedding. It must be really busy at the Congress right now. There will be so many papers to sign between both sides. You know Samuel is the President of the Continental Congress and they say he will be the President of the United States in Congress Assembled. From what Bob told us that shouldn't be long now. He wouldn't be able to leave his duties even for a short time.

We will have something for them here though. The friends we have around here will be invited including those of the Congregationalist Church. The Walkers are our relatives. When they came to live here they brought their beautiful Queen Anne highboy which they say will be passed down for generations. The Walkers also have the grist mill along with Mr. Landers and that is where we take our grain. We probably will not have room here at home for their reception but will have it at the church."

All the girls were so excited and they could hear the men in the other room planning on finishing the house and making plans to getting the barrels ready to pack with their products to go to the new U.S.A. It wasn't long until you could hear everyone bidding each other Goodnight and retiring to their rooms for the night with plans for a busy day tomorrow.

The day dawned bright and clear with everyone assuming their daily chores. Hannah was out gathering the eggs. Joseph was out milking the cows and the girls were making the breakfast. Sarah was already sketching the outfit she would make for Joseph. The men planned to get the fruit ready for shipment. They knew they would have time to finish the inside of the house after Bob was on his way to Connecticut with Joseph. After breakfast they were out in the orchards getting the apples ready for shipment. The barrels were all ready to pack. They hoped the ship was ready to go when Bob returned from visiting his family.

It was a week later when Bob arrived at their home. He looked so much better. They knew he missed his family when he was away from them and that he could catch up on his rest when he was home. Even Victory looked better for the rest. "I hope Joseph is ready for his trip, David," he said as he shook hands with his friend. "I could see at the barn you have all your produce ready to go. Someone will have to go with me and pull the wagon with all the shipment to load onto the sloop."

Joseph just then came out of the house. Bob could hardly recognize him. "Looks like I have another sailor here, David," he said as he walked around him. "If I didn't know better I would have thought I must have hired another hand. I see no danger of anyone recognizing him either here or in Connecticut."

You could tell Joseph was really pleased with Bob's comments. "Sarah just seemed to know what sailors wear and we could see her cutting and sewing for days to get the right affect." Joseph was proud of his sister.

"You are here early, Bob," David said. "I suppose you want to get an early start. The boys will come right out and load the wagon. Maybe you would like to come in and have a cup of coffee. I suppose you had breakfast but if not there is plenty for you. We already had ours."

"I think the men will be ready to start out, David. They had plenty of time to repair the ship. I want to see Susannah and the girls but then I should get on to start this trip. I hope we don't have any trouble but we have to be prepared." Joseph went out to help load the wagon and David welcomed Bob into his home. Susannah had a letter ready to send with Bob for the Connecticut family. She wanted to be sure they would all know that they would welcome Joanna into their family. They knew the love Joseph had for her and that they would love her also. The wagon was loaded and ready in no time. Bob made sure he bid everyone in the family good- bye and asked them to pray he would get through to Connecticut. Mammy was standing with them as Bob mounted Victory and the others all rode on the wagon to the sea where the sloop was docked.

Bob arrived first and found everything repaired and in good order. It wasn't long until everyone had boarded the sloop and the barrels were secure. The sailors were introduced to their new helper. Bob informed them all that he was just here with them for one trip and he would be training him to help them with the duties. Joseph could see that he really looked the part of a sailor and was again thankful to his sister for making the outfit. He also carried a gift to Joanna. He had her wedding slippers made by the cobbler and they were very colorful, each alike. They would fit on either one of her feet. Sarah had embroidered flowers all over them. Sarah had been very busy making all the clothing. She had also made the cloak for Joseph, his cravat, his cocked hat and breeches. She had knitted his hose which would cover his legs to the knee. His family would all see their wedding clothes at the reception his family would have for them when they returned. Anyway, he planned to enjoy this trip. It certainly would be better than the last trip he made by sea. Now he had the added blessing of reuniting with his sweetheart. He could hardly wait. They were off in no time and he stood with Bob as he stood at the helm of the ship. There seemed to be no disturbance at sea and so far it seemed like it would be a quiet trip. Bob hoped it would be. He didn't want to make the wrong choice in bringing Joseph along.

The weather cooperated and it was a good experience to work with these sailors. He had slept well all night and joined them in breakfast the next day. It wasn't long until Bob sighted land and a group of people waiting on the shore. "I think we have a welcoming committee, Joseph," he called out to him.

Joseph could see Uncle John standing there with his beautiful Joanna, her sister, Sarah, the twins, Mark and Thomas and then little Emma running from one to another. Joanna's hair was blowing in the wind. It had escaped from the bun she always put it in. He wondered how they could possibly know when they would arrive at the shore of Connecticut. Joseph was the first one to step on shore. He ran to Joanna and both of their faces were streaked with tears. They had waited so long but through the grace of God they were able to endure the wait. Everyone drifted away up the shore to give them the privacy they needed while the sailors and Bob secured the sloop.

"My darling, my darling, How I have longed for this day. I hope and pray that we will never be separated again." Joanna was speechless as she just looked up at Joseph with stars in her eyes. She loved him so very much.

They finally joined their family to go back to their home. Joseph joined the family in the wagon for the ride back. The apples had been unloaded from the sloop and they would be ready to return as soon as Bob was ready. The ship was not damaged this time which looked promising for a good trip back after the wedding. "Joseph," Joanna said. "I am all ready for the wedding. We will get married tomorrow if that meets your plans and then we will be ready to go."

"You know, darling, I am ready right now. Our families are so much alike. I am sure you will feel right at home when you arrive at Nova Scotia. Let's thank the Lord right now as we sit in this wagon."

Everyone was silent as they noticed Joseph and Joanna with their heads bowed in prayer. It was comforting to them all that their family was united in giving God thanks for everything.

The family was soon at their destination and sitting at the table for their dinner. The girls brought Joanna to her bedroom to show her the wedding dress her grandmother had made for her. Joanna was delighted with the dress. It was a dress she thought she would only be dreaming of. It was the most called for color of wedding dresses at this time. The blue was the color of the sky. When Joanna tried it on they couldn't believe the perfect fit of the dress. Grandma had even crocheted her a veil to go with it. Just then they heard a knock at the door. It was Joseph. They quickly tried to hide Joanna, all of them laughing.

"Joseph, go away," her sister Sarah said. "Don't you know that you are not supposed to see Joanna in her wedding dress until the time you see her coming down the aisle of the church? She will be out in a few minutes when she changes back into her other clothes."

Joseph did not open the door. "I wanted to give her the shoes I bought for her before I left Nova Scotia. Remember my sister, Sarah, did the decorations on them. I will go away and leave the shoes at the door." He put the shoes down at the door and walked away. It seemed like girls had so many odd ideas. All the wedding finery was put away and the girls came out of the room giggling. When Joanna tried on the shoes they were all excited about how beautiful they were and how they went with the dress and fit perfectly.

Joanna walked over to Joseph to thank him for the beautiful shoes. They sat down on the divan holding hands not wishing to be separated but her parents had different plans. It wasn't long until it was time to go to bed. They knew Bob and his family would be there early for the wedding as would all the guests.

"Joseph," Joanna's mother said, "You can sleep in Joanna's room and she will sleep in one of the girls' room. It will be an early breakfast and then you will both have time to get ready as we will also."

"Just one more night of separation. I guess we can get through that, honey," Joanna said as she squeezed his hand. Everyone said their good-nights and they were soon in their rooms to get some rest.

The sun was coming up when they started to get up from their rest and get ready for the wedding. Everyone ate a scanty breakfast. Joanna's sister, Sarah was excited about her place as the bridesmaid. Friends were completing the rest of the wedding party. John was ready to walk up the aisle with his daughter. He was pleased with her choice of a husband but he was sorry they would be so many miles away from them. He had prayed about it and knew they were blessed by God to spend their lives together.

The guests all arrived early and were seated at the church. The ladies at the church had planned a reception for them. Everyone was happy about the wedding and the state of the war right now. It was almost noon by the time the wedding was in process.

It was a beautiful wedding from the time John walked down the aisle with Joanna until the Pastor's remarks and the pronouncement that they were husband and wife. The reception followed and they were soon on their way to the sloop after changing to their sailor outfits. Amidst tearful goodbyes they were soon on their way. One sailor remarked that it looked like they had picked up another hand. Joanna looked the part. Bob's family was going back home. They were delighted to be invited to this wedding.

They didn't have the produce they usually had to deliver so there was room for them all on this trip. Joanna stood on the deck watching as the shore disappeared from view. She felt sadness along with her happiness to have Joseph by her side. She saw other ships in the distance and knew she had to play her part as a sailor so that they could have a safe trip to Nova Scotia.

When they arrived in Nova Scotia David, Susannah and their family were there to welcome them and thank God for the safe trip of their new family member. The next day the reception the family had prepared was ready and they all could celebrate the wedding of Joseph and Joanna. They put on the clothes they had worn for the wedding in Connecticut. Everyone was so happy for them and had joined with the family in providing the reception for them. The wedding cake was beautiful. There were so many good cooks and bakers in the church. After the reception David and Susannah told them they had a surprise for them. They took them to their new home. It was beautiful. It needed more furniture but the neighbors had helped furnish the home and gave their time to finish the inside of the house. Joseph and Joanna were so surprised at the wedding gift of their time and furniture. The bed was large and sturdy and when Joanna saw the bed she ran over to it because she noticed the beautiful quilt on the bed.

"The Martha Washington pattern, I am so pleased! Who made this quilt? Who made this quilt?" she asked as she just stood in awe of the beautiful workmanship.

"Joanna," Susannah said. "We wanted you to feel at home as much as possible. The girls and I worked on it and I'll tell you it was hard at times to hide the whole quilting frame from Joseph. We would constantly work on it and then see him out in the yard and quickly hide it again. Sarah did a lot of the designing."

Joseph came into the room and admired the quilt. "I thought there was something going on, Mother. Every time I came in it seemed like everyone was dashing here, there and everywhere. I was wondering what was going on. Thank you so very much. Joanna and I will value it for the rest of our life. So many times he had lost hope of ever seeing Joanna again in this life time. Then he would ask God's forgiveness for doubting His power to make all this possible. Praise God it had come about and they were together.

Joanna walked over to look at the scenery out of their window. She could see this was a beautiful country. It reminded her of the writing her Aunt had given her before she left Connecticut. As she looked out of their window she went over the words in her mind.

Change
There is something so comfortable about
The familiar,
The old,
And something so frightening about
The uncharted,
The new,
The different
Perhaps that is why
In the midst of change and uncertainty,
It is good to know,
That God who never changes,
Who loves me today
Just as He has in the past,
Provides Grace in this need also.
Setting my mind on this truth,
I look out my new window
At a new scene,
And lo, the sun still shines
And the world is beautiful here, too.

Epilogue

JOANNA STOOD AT HER favorite place in her beautiful home at the window overlooking the fields and orchards in the background. Her beauty still shone out as it had when she was first married in 1780. It was now 1783 and Joanna rejoiced as she had found out the war was over.

The treaties of Paris and Versailles were signed formally ending the war. On March 1, 1781, the Articles of the Confederation - the nation's first attempt at a constitution went into effect, officially transforming the 13 sovereign states into a single entity known as the United States of America. Uncle Samuel became the nation's first "real" president of the United States when his title changed from "President of the Continental Congress" to "President of the United States in Congress Assembled."

She cuddled baby John as he lay sleeping in her arms. She and Joseph had already dedicated him to the Lord at their church service. She looked back over her shoulder where she could see the American Flag by the fireplace and also the Connecticut flag. She wished she could be at her childhood home to celebrate with her family but she had been so happy here. She had felt right at home immediately at the Congregationalist Church where Joseph's family were members and even had a part in establishing the church. She had always felt God's love in her home and the love of Joseph and his family.

She looked at the flag of Nova Scotia and knew this was their home. She looked out of their window and knew her Aunt's poem had captured her feelings exactly.

About the Author

Jean Crawford lives in DeMotte, Indiana and is an active member of the DeMotte United Methodist Church. She is also a member of the Margaret Bryant Blackstone Chapter of the DAR in Hebron, Indiana. She previously lived in Florida for twenty three years and was a member of the Faith Bible Church in Deltona, Florida. She was also a member of the Gemini Springs Chapter of the DAR in Deltona, Florida.

Jean has previously written four books in The Quilted Story series. She holds a certificate of membership in the Newspaper Institute of New York City and has completed a course of writing at Daytona Beach College in Florida.

Bibliography

1. Books and Publications on History of the American Revolutionary War Era

   D'Agnese, Joseph and Kurman, Denise. Signing Their Lives Away. Philadelphia, PA: Quirk Books, 2009.

   McGovern, Ann. If You Lived in The Colonial Times. New York, NY: Scholastic Paperbacks, 1992.

   Roden, Philip. Life and Liberty/An American History. Glenview, Illinois: Sciott, Foresman and Company, 1984.

   Editors of Time-Life Books. The Revolutionaries. Alexandria, VA: 1996.

2. Quoted Works of Poetry

   Kraft, Louise. "Change."